Sophie is the ninth of eleven children born to Sarah Musanda, and the third of the five children born to Sarah and her second husband Daniel Chifuwe. She was born in Mukwela, a small suburban town in Zambia. At eight, she moved to Choma, where she completed both her primary and secondary school education before gaining entry to the University of Zambia College of Agriculture, NRDC. In 1988, the British Council offered Sophie a scholarship to study for a postgraduate diploma and a master's degree in agricultural extension. She is married with four children and two grandchildren.

This book is dedicated, first, to the late pastor Ernest Appleby of Mount Zion Assembly of God Church in Reading, who went to be with the Lord many years ago; second to my children and grandchildren, the best family I could ever ask for. You are my world and I love you all. You bring so much sunshine into my life. I cannot imagine life without your jokes and your unique ways. You make life worth living.

Sophie Scenic-Daniels

LIFE WITHOUT MY FAMILY – LONE SURVIVOR OF ELEVEN CHILDREN

Overcoming Grief with Faith

AUSTIN MACAULEY PUBLISHERS™

LONDON • CAMBRIDGE • NEW YORK • SHARJAH

A CIP catalogue record for this title is available from the British Library.

ISBN 9781788480901 (Paperback)
ISBN 9781788786980 (ePub e-book)

www.austinmacauley.com

First Published 2022
Austin Macauley Publishers Ltd®
1 Canada Square
Canary Wharf
London
E14 5AA

Table of Contents

Preface

I am writing this book to fulfil a promise I made to the late pastor Ernest Appleby, who was the senior pastor of the Mount Zion Assemblies of God church I attend in Reading. I made a promise to him to put my life story into a book to encourage readers to trust in God and never allow adversity or bereavement like it is with me to dictate how they feel or live their lives.

Little did I know that what started as a desire many years ago would one day materialise. Writing this book is my way of showing that encountering adversity at any stage in your life does not mean that hardships and pain will always brand your life, not at all. After one evening service, I sat by pastor Appleby on the right side of the church. I cannot recall how I came to share my desire to write a book with him. I guess I did it because I trusted him so much that I felt comfortable to tell him anything and everything that I felt he could advise me on. It may be because I wanted him to pray for me to start the project so that my book would turn out well. This is highly likely.

I can vaguely remember feeling so reassured by the few words he spoke in response to my request and thanking him as I left to go home. Whatever he may have said gave me so much reassurance that the fear and apprehension I felt before talking to him disappeared…

I do not remember him praying, but I remember him smiling and saying, "Go for it; God will be with you."

This was a highlight for me. As a young woman who had lost her father, any relationship with any real father figure meant a lot to me. Besides, this was a man of integrity whose character was unquestionable. Apart from that, his personal experience of tragedy, having lost his father at an early age and assuming responsibility for his family resonated with me as I had faced a similar situation, even though in my case, I did not assume full responsibility of taking care of my family following my father's untimely death. Like me, he had also lost a brother to tuberculosis and openly talked about it to his congregation. I rated his credibility among the top.

Many years have passed. Pastor Appleby is 'gone to glory, a term used to describe the death of a believer. The only downside of this phrase is that I denied him the pleasure of celebrating the result of his fatherly support and guidance to me since I did not get to write my book when he was still alive. It remained outstanding until now. Sadly, he's not here to read it and say a prayer of thanksgiving with me. I praise God; that I have finally found the courage and strength to write this very special book written in his honour. Because Pastor Appleby taught me the importance of openly sharing my pain with others, I am not afraid to share very personal things with myself and my family. I believe it is in being transparent about our feelings with others and speaking the truth about our life experiences to others, that we help them know that what they may go through is not unique to them, and that way, we become true encouragers.

Here is my book, twenty years on. Even though two decades have gone by, writing this book has been worth every minute I have spent doing so. I hope it will inspire readers because my story is the story of my personal encounter with adversity. It is a story of true Christianity and genuine faith in God. I share how knowing God helped me to embark on the journey of healing that I have been on for many years. I want readers to know that because of the grief I experienced after losing my parents and my siblings; I found hope in God and that hope has given me the strength I need to overcome all forms of adversity daily.

I know that this is the sort of triumph that God gives to those who believe in His words; those who call on Him for help. The God who has seen me through the dark season of my life will continue to be with me as I continue on my life's journey. I am persuaded that he can see me through all the challenges that may come my way. Knowing these things gives me greater hope, and it makes my desire to trust God even stronger. It gives me the strength to fight on until I finally leave this world for my heavenly home, which is my destination, and motivates me to encourage others to do the same.

I know, with no doubt that the God who has brought me this far will continue upholding me and showing me His grace, mercy and favour as I continue my life's journey until the day He takes me home to be reunited with the dear ones who went ahead of us all. I may have experienced deep personal losses and the pain that goes with it because of losing so many members of my family, so close and so dear to me, but only one thing matters and this is the fact that they may be gone, but I am still here, and I am grateful to God for that.

Instead of being bitter, I feel fortunate to still be here. I am grateful to God that despite everything I have been through so far in my life; my adversity has helped me to grow from strength to strength, God helping me. I put it all down to God's faithfulness and unfailing love. My prayer is that I will continue experiencing God's love, grace and favour for the rest of my life. It is my hope and prayer that other people who have a similar experience as mine can testify with me that God is truly faithful to those who put their trust in Him, no matter what life may throw at them.

I can honestly and boldly declare that I find strength and courage to carry on with life because of my faith in God. His word is powerful and living. This brings one of my favourite bible verses, which is found in Psalm 20:7, to my mind. It says;

"Some trust in chariots and some in horses,
but we trust in the name of the LORD, our God."
(Psalms 20:7) NIV

There is not any doubt that I am what I am today, and I have reached the stage I have reached in my life because of my faith. God is truly a God of love. He has been my present help and source of strength during the hard years of experiencing loss and bereavement, having lost nine siblings, my father and more recently my mother and the last sibling to go who passed away in 2012.

I am sure by now it is clear to the reader from the bible verse I have quoted that I am a born-again Christian. I find using bible verses to share my experience the best way. It tells the story of my life exactly. I want every reader to bear with me, please. You will come across bible verses throughout this book and my future publications. This is simply because the bible is an essential part of my life. It has made the biggest impact on me and it is therefore the only way I can share the story of my life and give my testimony more meaningfully.

My life is what it is today because I totally believe that the bible is the word of God and therefore; I believe everything written within it. I find reading and doing my best to apply what they wrote in the bible beneficial. Resorting to God's promises from the bible and following its principles at different times of my life has served me well. Although some read it as a storybook, it is a living testimony of Jesus Christ, the son of God, and the best manual for life. I have found it encouraging and its significant source of hope during times of uncertainty. It gives a special type of hope that makes challenges of life seem more bearable.

In using bible verses, I do not intend to put anyone off; rather, to provoke their curiosity about the BIBLE, the all-time best seller that has lifted the spirits of many a man and woman during dark and hopeless times; for instance, when facing death sentences and persecution, many have survived. To put it in simple terms, living by bible principles is like using a recipe book to make a cake. Just as it would be impossible to make the cake if any of the ingredients were missing or if they did not follow the method, it would be impossible to live a real Christian life without reading the bible. Finding peace and contentment in life does not come by attending church and praying without an understanding of bible principles. The bible is the best manual for life and from experience; it works. Trying to live life without paying attention to what the bible says is like trying to operate a piece of equipment without reading the manual.

Introduction

I Faced Adversity and Faith in God Helped Me Overcome This

It is inevitable for me to write this book both for the reader and for myself. It is my way of affirming my victory over adversity through faith in God and in Jesus Christ, his son, who is the author and finisher of my faith. I needed something to hold on to when I was going through grief for losing my father and seven of my siblings. As a young woman, I could not understand why there were so many deaths around me and I started fearing death. I surprise myself when I think about what I have been through and where I have got to in my life. If someone asked me to describe my life's journey, I would put it in one word; dramatic!

My mother lost seven children, then lost her husband, my father, but never blamed God. She instead lived a life of prayer, going to church and singing in the choir. She had no job, but somehow, she brought my three sisters and me up. We seemed to be scattered all over the place and never really got the chance to bond as sisters. With my mother's encouragement and support, I continued with my primary education after the death of my father until I went to secondary school and started spending holiday time, first with a cousin on my father's side and in later years with my brother from a different mother.

I became a Christian during my high school days. I went to a missionary school where attending church and singing hymns were a part of our daily routine. Saturday was the only day we did not need to go the church. The Methodist hymns we sang in assembly affected me. I sought God for myself and finally found Him through scripture union meetings and bible studies. This changed my life. It took away the emptiness I felt and gradually answered the questions I had about life. It changed the way I dealt with the pain of loss that I lived with for a long time and helped me to deal with other challenges I faced as a young woman differently. In this book, I am writing about the life lessons I learnt through pain and how going through pain does not exempt us from being our normal selves or free us from our duties and roles in the family, community, church or workplace. Also, we need to understand that unless they will help us, the chances that we continue sinking in despair are high. Unless we make up our minds not to let adversity defeat us, the chances of getting defeated are high. I share practical examples of how I dealt with different situations to show that, with time, things eased off.

After graduating from college, I got married and had four children. Although I went through difficult situations that no young woman wants to go through while I was at college, God brought me through them and gave me the strength to carry on. I know I have scars, but they are mere marks and constant reminders of what I went through.

Life as a Christian has not always been straightforward. There have been disappointments and heartaches along the way, but I cannot imagine life any other way. I have faced discouraging events, and I have felt rejected, but I know that even though fellow human beings are bound to cause us pain, God cares and He has a way of showing us His love just when we need Him. Despite graduating in agricultural science, I embarked on a career in social care and although it has not been easy; I do not regret the career change I made. It is one of the best decisions I have ever made. Things got tougher for me when I started undergoing career progression. As a black woman, rising to the position of Care Manager did not come without its challenges. However, because of my faith in God, the support of my family and other Christians, I kept my head above the waters and to this day, I still enjoy my social care career.

I ended up in one of the best schools in the country, did so well in my O-level examinations and entered the college of agriculture. All this time, none of my friends, teachers or lecturers had any idea who I really was and what pain I was carrying in my heart. I seemed to carry on with life as normal. To remain sane, I even played sports, competed for my hall, and won trophies. I attended church, joined dance clubs, and did everything other pupils and students did. But I was hurting. That made me sensitive. I felt vulnerable and easily withdrew at the appearance of any opposition. Nobody seemed to notice it, which I think was a good thing.

After completing college, I immigrated to the west. At this point, I had three children, having my fourth child after two years of living in the western world. By reading the bible and listening to the preachers of God's word, I have gained a deeper understanding of the promises in its pages. It has given me the strength to carry on. As a result, I have developed the strength not to let adversity destroy my future or steal my joy.

In hindsight, I can see what a symbiotic relationship we had with our teachers. They taught us and we benefited from their high standards of teaching. Our government needed them, employed them as expatriates, and paid them well. Everyone was pleased. There were no tensions of any kind and neither were there any insecurities on either side. It worked for both and both trusted the other. This is not the same feeling I get by being the foreigner in the country I currently live in. As an immigrant, there are times I feel as though I am not welcome in the country I have settled in. This is not a good feeling to have and the sad thing about it is that after spending over twenty years in a place, one acclimatises and no longer fits in when they try returning to their country of birth. For an African living in the west, there comes a time when the Western culture causes lifestyle changes, the development of new personal values, and a change in their bodies' ability to cope with the tropical climate. Their tolerance for the laid-back, easy-does-it way of life and attitude work becomes uncomfortable. After several years of living abroad, some reach a point of no return. The good news, however, is that there is in every human being the inert ability to adapt to suit whatever surrounding and situations they find themselves in. We are all amazing, though I therefore want to share the advantages of joining a missionary school where attending morning assembly, singing hymns and reading scriptures Monday to Friday before the beginning of the study day was compulsory. I found so much strength from the hymns we sang and found courage to deal with the pain of losing members of my family, especially my father. I joined the school a broken girl and lived a life of pain and sadness until I joined Njase Girls School, where I found the hymns and bible verses encouraging and motivating. They gave me a special hope and motivated me to carry on with my education despite the deep-seated grief that I lived with until I wrote and passed my O-levels.

I am so glad that I discovered the bible. It has been an enormous influence on the choices I have made and has shaped my character. By sharing bible verses and everything else that has influenced my choices, I hope readers can see how having personal values and a strong and living faith in God is necessary at every stage of one's life and critical during times of adversity. One's values and faith become the anchor that one needs to stand strong and remain steadfast when the going gets tough, just as the saying goes; when the going gets tough, only the tough get going. It takes the right attitude, personal values and faith in God to fight and refuse to give up, no matter how fierce the battle may get.

Although I share my faith widely throughout the book, I am not writing it just for Christians. I am writing it to anyone who is looking for answers to the challenges of life. This book is for anyone who has or may still experience grief and other forms of adversity. It is simply a record of how reading the bible and developing a strong faith in God can help with getting over dark periods in life; those periods when nobody cares and nobody really understands. Before cultivating strong faith in God, I also felt that nobody cared. I felt no one understood what I was going through and so no one could help me out. So, I turned to God and started reading about His promises. In Numbers 23:19, the bible says;

"God is not human, that he should lie, not a
human being, that he should change his mind. Does he speak
and
then act? Does he promise and not fulfil?"
(Numbers 23:19) NIV

Any Christian will be familiar with the bible and its applications. You know God speaks to His people primarily through His word, the bible, and He does this in a variety of ways. Sometimes he speaks through preachers, while other times he speaks directly while reading the bible and sometimes he speaks through prophets. I recall multiple instances in my life when bible verses jumped out at me as I read them. Occasionally, listening to a sermon felt like the preacher was speaking directly to me. Other times, I felt a great sense of conviction when I was praying or meditating.

This is a common occurrence of what I go through during periods of praying and fasting when seeking God for solutions and asking Him for directions. I can confidently say that time and time again, holding on to a bible promise helped me to see a light at the end of the tunnel and kept me going when the going got tough. I am so glad that I learnt to read the bible and to pray because without these, I may not have been alive today.

I love going to church and always look forward to a time of singing hymns and choruses. I developed the habit while I was at boarding school. To this day, hymns and choruses have continued, time and time again bringing me hope. They never cannot remind me of God's love and faithfulness, and this helps to heal. I don't want quick fix or short-lived solutions; these would not be enough to take away the deep-seated and long-standing pain of losing my dear ones and to keep me going. I thank God that, although the journey has been slow, and not without twists and turns, I have gained momentum with age, and a closer walk with God that came about through reading the bible and praying, just like the praying mother who brought me up and taught me how to live for God.

I am a living testimony of how God answers prayers; otherwise, I may not have been alive today. That has motivated me to write this book to reassure the reader that life does not stop when we lose those who are dear to us. It starts there. It may be necessary to adjust certain aspects of our lives to fill gaps left by our dear ones, but life goes on. This is the reason we should not allow bitterness and anger to take hold of us. It would be pointless. We need to ask ourselves this question; will my anger bring my dead family back? Is it going to make me feel better? Will my anger help me? Think about it and make necessary amends.

It is so true that adversity has helped me to develop in character and has made me a hard nut to crack. It has given me the much appreciated and crucially necessary life experience that has helped me to develop ways of applying my faith in God to circumstances that confronted me and has made me stronger when dealing with adversity. I have learned, and I know from experience that if God is on one's side, victory is sure. I know this is easier said than done, but it is the truth, speaking from experience. Grief is painful. There is no easy way out for those stricken by it. It is therefore important that when going through grief, we try our best to do everything to fight on our own; it can be done. No need to throw in the towel. Try faith in God like I did. If it worked for me, I have no doubt that it can work for anyone. God is patient. He never gives up on anyone just like these verses put it;

"28. Do you not know? Have you not heard? The Lord is the everlasting God, the Creator of the ends of the earth. He will not grow tired or weary, and his understanding no one can fathom. 29. He gives strength to the weary and increases the power of the weak."
(Isaiah 40:28–29) NIV

These verses mean a lot to me. I understand God is who He says He is; the everlasting God through adversity. I sank to a very low place in my life after the death of my father. But God restored me. He has been healing me and is still working on me patiently. Instead of finishing me, adversity has built my inner strength. I can say that it has done me so much good by giving me a cause to fight every step of the way. With God's help, I am determined to do everything; I cannot allow the pain and grief I have suffered to make me bitter or to cause me to blame God. Instead, I will do everything I can to live a life of love; go so far as loving even those who do not find me loveable for whatever reason.

My personal tragedy has helped me to understand that man has very little control over events that come his way. I have also come to this conclusion that there are only two ways of dealing with tragedy; adopting the victim mentality and suffering the consequences of that choice or adopting a winner mentality that says, 'It does not matter what life throws at me, I will not lose hope. I will forever remain grateful to God for sparing my life. I am still here; I could easily have been the dead one. For that reason, I will always trust God and believe His living word. I will stand on every bible promise I come across that relates to my situation. I am determined to try my level best to turn things around with God's help and by doing so, frustrate the plans of the enemy who the bible says, he comes not, but to kill, steal and destroy, to rob me of my life and to steal my future. It will not happen if God is still on the throne. He has the final say to every matter.'

Being bereaved does not exempt anyone from the demands of a normal life. It is so important to understand that life will go on. Unfortunately, bills will have to be paid even during our period of grieving. One must attend work or college or other vocational commitments to survive. This is because grief does not earn us the privilege to be exempt from living a normal life, carrying out everyday life activities and maintaining relationships with others. It makes it a lot harder to relate to other people like everyone else. The period of grief warrants us special terms for existence or replaces the need to remain accountable for various tasks and activities of daily living. There's still an expectation for us to play our part to keep the family and ourselves going. We do not cease being members of our churches or our local communities at all and neither does it stop you from experiencing normal things people go through every day. We remain subject to all the stages of life human beings go through and face the same challenges everyone faces at different stages of their lives.

However, it does change your outlook to life and makes you a lot more sensitive and alert. You still need to go to school, college, look for and find a job after college. You still need to socialise, find love, get married and start a family for those that need to. You still need to perform satisfactorily in your job role to keep your job and get promotion. You still need to attend church and clubs like everyone else and the expectation is that you behave just like everyone else regardless. People may not even know your story and for all I know, they may not care even if they did. So, you might as well accept the fact that there will be moments when you will feel all alone, when nobody seems to understand you and it's during moments like these when it will hurt the most and even drive you to withdraw to a lonely place which might feel safer. This is okay. Just make sure you fight and rise from those dumps and put on a brave face until you regain your confidence to carry on and socialise with others. All in all, bereavement does not make you immune to life principles, challenges and the highs and lows.

However, it changes your outlook on life and makes you a lot more sensitive and alert. The need to go to school or college still stands. You still need to find a job and perform to the expected standard. Bereavement does should not stop us socialising, finding love, getting married and starting a family if you are at that stage of life like I was. Your employers will expect you to perform satisfactorily in your job role to keep your job and get a promotion if that is your goal. You still need to attend church and clubs like everyone else, and the expectation is that you behave just like everyone else, regardless. People may not even know your story and for all I know, they may not care even if they did. So, you might as well accept the fact that there will be moments when you will feel all alone, when nobody seems to understand you and it's during moments like these when it will hurt the most and even drive you to withdraw to a lonely place which might feel safer. This is okay. Just make sure you fight and rise from those dumps and put on a brave face until you regain your confidence to carry on and socialise with others. Bereavement does not make you immune to life principles, challenges, and the highs and lows.

Chapter 1

Early Life

As a young man, my father, Mr. Daniel Palicha Chifuwe, was a Zambia Railways labourer, but he resigned from his position with the company at an early age to become a butcher. Being an industrious and hardworking man, he somehow made what could have been a tough decision to leave the national railway company to work for himself; I guess as a way of improving his standard of living and preparing a better future for his children. I can clearly remember him always wearing a black suit, a black hat and a tie, pottering the streets, either visit pubs and telling people about God or networking with Asian merchants, farmers, government officials and church leaders. He also enjoyed discussing ideas for developing his community.

My Father Was the Driving Force Behind the First School to Be Built in His Area

My father was such an industrious man who believed in community development. It's no wonder he was the driver behind the setting up of the first primary school in a small rural area of the southern province of the southern African country where I grew up. Until my father pioneered the school, there was no nearby school for the children who lived in the area to attend to. Dad had to no other option but to send my older siblings to members of his family scattered all over the southern province whenever they attained the school age. It did not impress my father that there was no nearby school for his children to attend, as he believed in education and wanted all his children to get an education, whatever it took. He did not want to wait for someone else to do something about it.

By the time I reached the right age for starting school, my father had pioneered the first school in the area and had gone so far as organising contractors to put up the first building. This meant that I did not have to leave home when it was my time to start school, like my older siblings did. I may not have realised what a blessing it was for me to attend a local school and be able to continue living at home with my parents. By this time, I had no clue what fate awaited the family. I just carried on with my life like any other school-age child, not expecting my father, a hard-working and family-oriented man, a key figure in his community to lose his life on 13 September 1976, in his forties. This was an enormous blow to me and the rest of my family. But how could a successful man and key figure in his community die just like that? What about his family? What about me? A daughter he was so proud of because I had always come top of my class in year-end exams. Who was going to hold my hand and walk to the nearby shop which used to belong to his cousin to buy me sweets to reward me for a job well done in my exams? What did life hold ahead for me, my mum, and my siblings?

When My Father Died, a Girl of About Six or Seven Jeered at Me

I will never forget an encounter I had with some of the children in my school when my dad died. To protect us from the impact of mourners wailing and rolling on the floor, a display often seen at Southern African country funerals, my mum and other family members sent us off to school even before my father's committal, but this was a grave mistake. I can remember one girl who was about my age laughing at me when she heard that my dad had died.

She found it funny and mocked me as if to say, serves you right; who is going to be showing you off, now that your dad who used to do it each time you came first in class has died? I remember removing myself from the scene as I could not bear to hear anymore unkind words from this girl or anyone else for fear that they may carry on laughing when all I really needed was someone to console me for my pain having just lost my dad. Does the bible not say in Jeremiah 17:9 that:

> "The heart is deceitful above all things,
> and beyond cure. Who can understand it?"
> (Jeremiah 17:9) NIV

There are some unkind people in this world, and they thrive on seeing others suffer. How could a child as young as six or seven be so cruel? I know for sure that they did not know how deeply hurt I already was and how their words added salt to my wound. Sadly, my encounter with this girl was not an isolated one. Through the years, I have come across many more people who seem to thrive on other people's pain, at least and I think I am entitled to one although in my case, I need to be careful since in Christian circles, it's not one's opinion that matters, but what God says in His word. It appears as if some of those people who seem to thrive on the pain of others wait until you feel most vulnerable before they strike. It's usually their choice of words that inflicts further pain on an already wounded person. What is sad is that some of these people are church-going, bible-believing Christians and I am speaking from experience.

Am I being judgmental by writing such a statement about my fellow Christians? I do not believe I am. However, I have since realised that although it felt at the time that I was being targeted, maybe I was not, as do not have any proof that I was. The issue is that since some of the Christian I interacted with had never been through what I had been through; it was more a case of them being insensitive and careless in their choice of words. I used to wonder how a Christian can be without compassion when the bible says so much about it?

People who normally come across as aggressive, patronising, oppressive and just unkind are, in most cases, not pastors. They may be older Christians with some sort of position in the church or organisation if this involves a work environment. It may just be a weakness of theirs and the only way to overcome this is to maintain your love and giving them due respect knowing that even Jesus, your saviour, suffered at the hands of religious leaders. His followers and even His own brothers questioned him, but He never gave up on them or disowned them. Remember, love wins.

A Christian blog I read describes compassion beautifully. It says that compassion is deeper and more profound than kindness and sympathy. The word originates from the Latin, word 'compati' which means 'suffer with'. Compassion means someone else's heartbreak becomes your heartbreak. Another's suffering becomes your suffering. Genuine compassion changes the way we live.

I couldn't agree more with the definition of compassion I read from a Compassion UK website that went something like this; true compassion changes the way we live. It changes us from being self-centred and ignores the pain of those around us by helping them experience healing because of the compassion we show them, instead of them getting worse to where they develop anger and hatred. When we exercise compassion and do everything, we can within our power to stand by those who may go through difficult times regardless of the reason behind their challenge. This way, we can help to bring healing. When we treat others with compassion, we deactivate the energy of anger and frustration that has frequently driven some people to commit murder because they had not dealt the anger in them with.

I can only imagine that if the Lord had not healed me from the pain that I suffered when I was most vulnerable and emotionally unstable, I would be a bitter and angry person today. This would have stopped me from achieving the little I have achieved so far in my life. Although it is not within my character to wish anyone any harm or even think of picking up a gun and shooting someone literally, I could probably have been walking about harbouring bitter envy and avoiding those who fit the description of my tormenters. What would I have gained from that sort of attitude? Nothing, except for more and more pain and possibly the illnesses that go with it. I could have been a prisoner of my mind. That would have incapacitated me and prevented me from benefiting from fellowshipping with other Christians and thoroughly enjoying their company.

A good example of how anger can lead to murder happened to a medical doctor in England nearly ten years ago when he murdered hundreds of his unsuspecting patients before one of his patient's daughters uncovered his secret many years later. Patients and the families of the deceased became suspicious. Before long, someone within the system who noticed that his patients were dying at an alarming rate and seemed to die in the same way took action. According to an article published in a local paper, a local radio held a debate to discuss the motives behind this general practitioner's murders.

The article that was published in the paper on this case read; 'Although Dr White's (not his real name) motives remain unclear, he may have harboured a deep-seated need to control people and events. He may have had unresolved feelings about his mother's death when he was a teenager, yet they were not enough to explain his later conduct.'

Never allow grief to make you shut down, because the outcome of doing so could be dire. This brings me back to the questions I asked about my father's premature death. They are the sort of questions anyone who has lost a loved one pre-maturely would ask. They are the sort of questions that come from a broken soul and the type that there may be no answers to. The fact remains that different people react differently to loss. Some people express the pain of the dreadful experience of losing a dear one by shutting down and wishing they were dead, while others fight every negative thought that they may feel knowing that if they didn't, such thoughts have the potential to cause them emotional breakdown from which many never to recover from.

I know a man who never recovered from the loss of his elderly mother until he took his own life many years later. This man's death still pains me as I do not know what state his soul was when he died. When he visited my church, I sang a solo as I am in the habit of doing so during the evening services. When he heard me, he told my pastor and his wife to get me to sing an amazing grace at his funeral. Little did I know that he had been trying to find a way of ending his life for a while because he could not get over the death of his elderly mother. Different people react differently to loss.

I did sing at his funeral but that did not take away the pain I felt when I found out the way his life ended. It just points to the fact that as Christians, we need to be sensitive to the needs of people around us and pray to God to reveal to us what the future may hold for them so that we can try to support them, show them compassion and do what we can within our power to encourage healing. I am sure, that I would have prayed for this man's salvation more passionately had I known what was around the corner for him. But God knew, so it is well.

This is just one of the many stories of people who have followed their deceased relatives to the land of no return partly because there isn't enough support for people going through extended periods of bereavement. Although there are several bereavement counselling forums out there, they do not meet everyone's needs in full because the type and level of counselling offered may not be suitable for everyone. Sad to say that not even the church is fully equipped for this kind of service especially for those members who do not attend church regularly because if they did, the chances that the pastor would pick up on their struggle with grief would be much higher. In most cases, pastors and their wives find themselves bearing the burden of supporting bereaved members of their churches without much support from the rest of the members.

I know a man who never recovered from the loss of his elderly mother until he took his own life many years later. This man's death still pains me as I do not know what state his soul was in when he died. When he visited my church, I sang a solo as I am in the habit of doing so during the evening services. When he heard me, he told my pastor and his wife to get me to sing an amazing grace at his funeral. Little did I know he had been trying to find a way of ending his life for a while because he could not get over the death of his elderly mother. Different people react differently to loss.

Having experienced grief, a hundred times over myself, I have concluded that as grief is a deep seated, negative and painful inner emotion, not every counsellor has the right skills for getting to the very bottom of it and to address it suitably to bring relief to the bereaved person. It requires time and patience on the side of both the counsellor and the client. It also requires the commitment of both the client and their counsellor as well as building of trust, openness and willingness for the client to share how they feel each step of the way.

One thing that surprises me about myself to this day is how I have never, at any point during the period of my grief, ever questioned God or felt anger towards Him. I have one confession to make in line with that. One day, many years after the death of my father, the spirit of grief caught up with me. I wondered why my father and eight of my siblings had to die so early? My father was in his forties, six of my siblings as toddlers and two as young women in their thirties and forties.

After this happened, I had a strange dream at night. I dreamt that a man held my hand and led me to a poultry house to show me the chicken life cycle. He first took me to an incubator full of eggs about to hatch.

Then he said to me, 'What do you see?'

I said eggs. Then he said look carefully and tell me what else and I repeated the same answer as before, eggs. I could see when I looked for the third time that the layers had crushed some eggs, but before I could say anything, the man took my hand and led me to a coop where he showed me yellow chicks in their thousands. He asked me to look carefully and tell him what I saw. On looking closely, I noticed some chicks had stepped on had died.

Then he took me to the next poultry house full of full-grown chickens and asked me the same question; 'What do you see?'

My answer was, 'Full grown chickens.'

The man then said to me; 'Just as you have seen broken eggs, so they had no chance of ever hatching into chicks, and the dead chicks which had no chance of growing into fully grown chickens, it is the same with human life. Some people die in the womb, others die at birth, and others die as toddlers. There is nothing anyone can do about it. Not the most powerful scientist, not the richest man in the world, or the greatest preacher and faith healer.'

He said that this was because life and death were a mystery that only God had power over.

The strange thing about this dream is that although I was aware of a man holding my hand, I did not look at him to see his face. I could, however, clearly remember the entire dream as if it had happened yesterday. When I reflected on this dream, the only conclusion I come to is that, truly, only God has control over the mystery of life and death and man should therefore never question Him. It explains the reason since death entered humanity, countless numbers of people have been experiencing it left right and centre, and no one has ever found a solution to it; not the most advanced medical systems of the western world, or indigenous and traditional healers; no one can stop people dying.

The young, the old, the rich, the poor, the black, yellow, brown and white are all destined for the grave even though there has been a phenomenon of medical breakthroughs in contemporary times that have prolonged many lives. However, the fact remains that no ethnic group, social class, political party, or religious group is immune to death; everyone ends in the grave no matter who they are.

The Bible talks about death in the book of Hebrews, chapter nine verse 27 where it says:

"[27]Just as people are destined to die once, and after judgement," (Hebrews 9:27) (NIV)

And so, if all men have an appointment with death, then we should all be doing everything we can within our power to prepare for it. As no one knows their death day or hour, everyone should live as if they will die tomorrow and work hard to improve themselves and leave an inheritance for their children as if the world will never come to an end. Every day should be a day to make necessary amends, to do better in every aspect of one's life, to love and not hate, to help others and set goals and be focused on implementing these goals as if time was short, bearing in mind nobody knows how much time they still have in this life.

Even though I have every reason in the world to be bitter and angry with God, I have never been, and I never will. It reminds me of what I heard a female western pastor talking about: how she married a respected preacher not knowing he had HIV. When he passed away, he left her and her children behind. Instead of blaming God, she says in a documentary watched by many throughout the world that God is fair. How could she still say God is fair given her experience knowing it was not her fault that she married a sick man who died and left her to bring up her children as a single parent?

This makes little sense, especially if you look at it from a non-Christian point of view, which does not take into consideration the bible principle of forgiveness. I can only imagine that this lady could boldly say that God is fair only because He spared her life and those of her children from HIV-AIDS and from death. God had her and her children's best interest at heart. He gave them a new husband, a father, a loving man.

This woman's story has challenged me to rethink my attitude towards injustice. It has helped me to trust God in every situation; even in circumstances that appear as her late husband had lied to her and married her by deception. This shows that God is aware of what we may go through and He can make things good for us. We only need to trust Him to make it good for us because He is able. In the book of Romans 8: 28, the bible says:

"[28] And we know that in all things God works
for the good of those who love him, who[a] have been
called according to his purpose." (Romans 8:28) (NIV)

Things are working together for my good despite my traumatic early life. There is not any doubt that even in the death of my father and my siblings, all things have worked out for my good because, as already mentioned in earlier chapters, I love God and I know He has called me according to His purposes. Between losing my father, my siblings and the present moment, God has blessed me with four children of my own; two and two grandchildren, two adopted children who we have brought up as part of us. My two grandchildren from my first son Dan and two from my daughter Kantu, my nieces and nephews, great nieces and nephews who I love dearly and mean the world to me.

Good friends make such a big difference. God has blessed me with friends; many who are just like my blood sisters. Katarina Dryer, my best friend from secondary school who is just like my sister. I will never forget the re-union we had in 2016 when I visited the country where she currently lives in having not seen her for seventeen whole years. It was surreal!

My friend, who is as good as a sister, Joy Reid, someone I got so close to when we met in England, where she and her late husband, Mr. Able Sialwiindi came ahead of me in 1997 before I joined them the following year. My relationship with her was one of the strongest girlfriend relationships ever. People within our circles used to describe us as the twin sisters joined at the hip.

I cannot find the right words to use in describing the relationship that I have with a very special friend and prayer partner, Prudence Mwanza, a woman of focus and a strong family-oriented individual. These three women sit at the top of my friend's list. For those I live in the same country with, we did and still do many things together, like pray for one another and talk for hours on end by telephone and face to face now and again, regardless of the distance between us. We even travel together now and again and enjoy each other's company. The best part of my relationship with these women is our prayer partnerships. We have seen God turn many situations around in answer to our prayers over the years. I am forever grateful to God for bringing these dear women into my life.

I know there are many more very dear friends. If I were to include all the stories about my relationship with all my friends, this book will take forever to complete, will be too long and a tall order for some readers to finish reading it. How could I forget my friend Jean Bishop, now late, a cheerful and loving soul, Carla Alves, a beautiful woman, a loving mother and a lover of life? She is outgoing and friendly, not afraid to meet and befriend strangers on holiday. My dear friend Dr Carol Brickley, an intelligent and beautiful woman with a PhD in IT, she is such fun to be around. Pat Stewart, a hard-working and gentle soul, a loving person, and so much more. I count it as a great blessing to have them all as Christian friends and prayer partners. Each of these women have added great value to my life and have continued being sources of encouragement, courage and strength to bear the burden of grief throughout the time we have been friends some just by being there to share a cup of coffee and do girlie things and laugh. I can confidently vouch that spending time with friends is one of the best therapies for bereavement. It helps take one's mind off low moments, which are an inevitable part of grieving. I have had so many great friends with whom I have had great times, so much that mentioning them will take away the reader's focus from the subject of bereavement, which is the sole purpose of writing this book.

There's something about knowing you can count on some people. I say this from experience. Amongst my dear friends, there are some I can count on come rain some sunshine. They are happy to be inconvenienced, ready to jump in and support me anytime. As you can expect, I also have friends who only seem to want my company in times of sunshine, but not during dark moments. It is during difficult times when you know who your genuine friends are, but those who just want what they can get out of you will disappear. As the saying goes, 'Once beaten, twice shy, we therefore learn vital lessons about genuine friendship and know what to expect to avoid disappointments.'

Saying that, as a Christian, I know I have an obligation to love even those who don't treat me well and to support them if they need my support as opposed to the popular phrase; 'Revenge is sweet, but not so to a Christian, as revenge is not Christ-like.' I love all my friends and enjoy their company. They all make my life worthwhile and teach me to be strong, whether by being there for me or otherwise. I count myself very blessed to be a member of the UK Alumni of my former school, Njase. I enjoyed getting together with members of the committee as we always had fun when we met for business. The UK founder, Sarah Tembo and her confidant Ann Hamusankwa, two driven women with a passion to see the dilapidated infrastructure of our former school improved by funding refurbishment work with money raised through fund-raising events solely for the school. One ex-teachers of Njase, Miss Lorrayn de Peyer, has been a significant support to us during fund-raising. I pray to God to bless her for the relentless support she has rendered us in our fund raising efforts for Njase, our former school.

As a group of former Njase students, a couple of years ago, we organised a successful fund-raising event with Lorrayn's support. This took place at the seaside town of Devon where Lorrayn lives. The event attracted a few choirs which Lorrayn works with, alongside Mr and Mrs Norris, also former Njase teachers, now retired and back in England. It was such a great evening. That night, all the Njase girls joined Lorrayn and the Norris' on the podium to sing songs produced by Mr and Mrs Norris to raise more funds for our school.

The event was so well attended and a great success such that Sarah, our chairperson visited the school and bought materials to start the refurbishing work. As former Njase girls in the diaspora, we are determined to raise enough funds to complete refurbishing our school. We want to play our part in contributing to development efforts back home. I recall the points I made in the introductory page of my book; that experiencing grief does not exempt us from living normal lives and doing all the normal things that need doing, whether for our benefit, the benefit of our remaining family or that of our communities. I am a member of many charities. I am a part-time student, a mother, grandmother, an aunt, a friend, a church member, businesswoman and an employee, but I have no choice but to do all that needs doing to satisfy these different aspects of my life because being bereaved does not exempt me from the responsibilities of life. That gives me the determination to work hard. It also makes me grateful to God for sparing my life and for every opportunity to serve humanity in every way possible.

Chapter 2

The Blessing of Being Brought Up by a Praying Single Mother

After my father's committal, my mother needed to adjust from just being a dedicated wife and mother to being both a mother and father to us. She had to learn ways of generating income to feed and clothe her three younger children who were still at home with her; my late elder sister, Elizabeth Masusu, my late young sister, Eliya Jane and myself. This, I can imagine must have been hard for my mum, and so I commend her for not giving up, knowing that had she given up, my sisters and I would have been grossly affected and may have suffered irreparable emotional and mental breakdown considering we were also grieving the loss of our father.

To fend for us, my mother started a business, which entailed travelling to a riverside district of the southern part of the country, 82 miles away from her hometown, where she had moved after my father's death. This business meant that my mum would spend at least one month at the riverside in order to buy enough fish from the fishermen. She would disappear for a month at a time and spend time with other fish mongers and the fishermen. Gathering enough fish to take back home entailed waiting for the fishermen, who would disappear when the night got darker, and would return to the river bank at daybreak to find my mum and other fishmongers waiting to buy the fish off them. My mother and other fish mongers would then buy the fishes and start cleaning them right away to stop them rotting. They would then either sun dry or smoke them so that they could keep them until their return home, where they were to be sold.

My mother would then carefully stack her fishes on a bed made from dry twigs, grass and straw, which allowed the air to circulate around the fish to prevent them from rotting. Upon her return from the riverside, she would normally find the neighbours ready to buy the dried fishes off her immediately. That was a highlight because Mum would make more money from it, which kept us going for a while. She would do this at least three times a year during the school holidays, as she never wanted to leave home during the school term to ensure that she was around to get us ready for school and make sure there was food when we came back. I cannot remember who she left us with when she went away on her fish trading mission. She either left us on our own, or maybe requested the neighbours to watch over us.

Mum put us first. Getting re-married was not on top of her agenda. I can remember her trying to resettle by accepting to marry Mr Banda introduced to her by church friends who they purported to be a Christian, that being the only way my mum would have entertained the thought of marrying him. All I can remember about Mr Banda is him sitting by the fire, teaching us Chichewa Christian songs because he was a Chewa man from Malawi. I think my mum tried changing him into a genuine man of God, trying to make him like my father, who would lead us in prayer and get us singing hymns to God almost every evening. It never worked.

To this day, I can still remember most of the beautiful tunes this man taught us, which we continued singing even when he'd left my mum. My mum's brief marriage to Mr. Banda never worked for reasons best known to her and her husband of a few months. All I can think of is that he may not have been the right man for my mother, who needed a man that would provide her the spiritual nourishment and encouragement she desperately needed. I suspect also that my mum felt she needed to give us her undivided attention, and therefore had to make the difficult, but swift, decision to end the marriage without telling us.

One of the most cherished memories of growing up with Mum was hearing her praying in my sleep in the middle of the night. As a young girl, I couldn't work out what she was pulling down whenever she was in prayer. I used to hear her saying, 'I bind every stronghold of the enemy and pull down every evil thing lurking around and flying in the air in Jesus's name.' It wasn't until I grew up and read Matthew chapter 18:18 that says:

> "Truly I tell you, whatever you bind on
> earth will be bound in heaven, and
> whatever you lose on earth will
> be lost in heaven."
> (Matthew 18:18) (NIV)

My mum was a prayer worrier; thank God for that. I later understood that my mother was exercising the authority given to her by God when she became a Christian. Today, I understand the authority of a believer and I also exercise it at different times in different situations. I find God's generosity towards humanity amazing. I find it even more amazing that when I use the authority of God's word for different situations; it has worked. As a Christian, you will get answers to your prayers if you apply the right scripture in the right way at the right time. If you are not a Christian, you can still use scriptures to pray, to ask God for forgiveness, and to invite Jesus into your heart. You can also ask him to fill you with the Holy Spirit. I have seen it work many times and I'm sure it will work for anyone who prays in faith.

Another very interesting experience I had while being looked after by my single mother was when I earned a place at one of the best girls' boarding in Zambia-Njase, a highly sort after girls' boarding in 1975. Both my mother and I were very excited about the prospect of me attending such a famous and top-rated girls' school, but we both knew that it would not be easy to raise the school fees for me. My mother wrote to her young brother, my uncle Lot, who had immigrated to Malawi where he worked as a police officer asking for financial support. Although my uncle could not afford to pay my fees from his policeman's wages, he wanted to help my mother and therefore sold his motorbike to raise my first school fees and sent it to my mother.

Unfortunately, my uncle sent the money through his older brother, another of my mother's younger brothers, but he never passed the money to mum but used it. This devastated both my other and I. By now, the time for me to leave home for Njase was fast closing in. My mum, who had a thing about education, was not about to give up; no way was she going to let me miss the golden opportunity. I had to gain a qualification and have a bright future.

I can remember her approaching one leader of her church that used to work in an Indian supermarket and seemed to earn a lot of money, judging by the size and type of house his family lived in. I think that this man agreed to lend my mum some money, but only in part because the next day, I packed my suitcase and set off for the school with my mum.

I did not understand why my mum wanted to come all the way to the school but later realised that she wanted to negotiate with the then headmaster of Njase to accept the part payment she had raised while she found the rest of my fees. I can remember that on arriving at the school, my mum told me to wait outside the headmaster's office while she talked to him in confidence. Within a short time, I saw my mum walk out of the headmaster's office right past me, as I was still sitting outside the office on the visitor's bench. I suspect from the way she walked away from me without saying goodbye, that after stating her case to him, she did not want to give him any chance to disagree with her and so wanted to get away as fast as she could.

Soon, I would get passed to the head girl of the school to take me to my dormitory and show me my locker and my bed. In the meantime, I had an excruciating pain in my right toe because of a stud that had pricked me days before coming to Njase. I don't remember telling the head about my painful toe, but managed can remember her arranging for me to attend the clinic within the school grounds where I received treatment even before I attended my first lesson.

My mum raised the school fees for my first year. Before the end of the year, my late cousin Samuel Siamatendu, who was the named executor of my father's estate, agreed to support me when he heard my mum had paid my first year's fees. From then on, I started spending my school holidays with Sam and his family. His daughter Clara also went to Njase, although for a brief period, and left after one year. My cousin was a respected member of his community, a successful farmer who ran the village shop and owned cars. Although I felt welcomed and loved by his family, I missed my mum and so I made sure that I went to visit her during the school term as often as I could.

My mother missed my dad and talked about him a lot. That did not really help me let go of the pain of losing him, especially when I found myself surrounded by friends whose dads were still alive. Even though I had no issues with my friends who still had fathers, I missed mine and never really understood why he had died so early. I always had memories of him doing different things with the family and with me on a one-to-one basis. This brought a level of comfort and joy, but it would always fade faster that it would come. I think it made my mother turn to God, knowing her husband would never come back to earth. She always talked about looking forward to meeting him again in heaven when she died. One thing that still baffles me to this day is how my mum seemed so comfortable about the thought of death. My dear always wished that any illness she suffered would take her out. She almost always believed she was going to die each time she became ill. She always said she was ready to be reunited with her husband.

It never really dawned on me how much she believed in life after death. Her eagerness to die made me wonder how much she loved us? If she so wanted to be out of this world, but in hindsight, I think her faith in God gave her hope that if she died when she wanted to, God would have taken good care of us. There is a positive side to this; she only started talking about joining her husband in the sky after all her girls were in their twenties and thirties. She must have felt that she had done her part to raise us and give us an education each.

Throughout my secondary school years and beyond, my mother prayed for all of her children daily. She seemed to love reading the bible, telling neighbours about God and attending church three times a week; twice on Sunday and once on Wednesday. My mum's main prayer was for our protection. She seemed to travail in prayer for God to keep us safe, as if we were in some sort of danger. I know she believed God was watching over us through her prayers and she always made sure that we all attended church wherever we were because she believed it was only God who had the power to protect us from the danger seen or unseen.

The best part of being at Njase during my time was meeting and becoming a close friend of a new girl in the school, who had an anointing I had seen nothing like before. That was a good thing because that's what I needed, the type of Christianity that even grief-stricken girls like me benefited from. The newcomer's arrival revolutionised our school's scripture union to the disgust of the then headmaster and the then school chaplain. She brought hope to many girls who were struggling with different challenges of life. There's no doubt that my days at Njase played a pivotal role in reinforcing my Christian faith. It was at Njase that I became a born again Christian and got filled with the Holy Spirit. There is a verse in the bible that explains being born again, which is John 3:3 that says:

"3. Jesus replied, 'Very truly I tell you,
no one can see the kingdom of God
unless they are born again.'" (NIV)

God planned my meeting with Patrice, now a married woman, who at the time had been going through bereavement after losing her father, just like me by making her change schools and bringing her to my school to complete the last two years of her secondary education. He used her to revolutionise the school's scripture union and lead many girls to Christ.

Many girls spoke in tongues for the first time because of her. The anointing she carried was nothing like I had seen before. A good example of the impact her anointing carried was when she opened her mouth to pray during a normal scripture union meeting. Those in attendance received the Holy Spirit and spoken in unknown tongues. People cried uncontrollably until the school chaplain stopped the meeting and pulled Patrice to the side and ordered her not to pray like that again because she was causing confusion.

News of this occurrence spread throughout the school. As you can expect, there wasn't enough room to hold the number of girls that turned up for the next scripture union meeting in the usual room, so they moved the meeting to the dining hall. By this time, the school authorities were concerned. Nobody could work out what was going on and few had this sort of experience before, not even I. The meeting in the dining hall saw many nearly the entire school and God still turn. Again, when this girl prayed, the Holy Spirit came down and fell on those in attendance. There was nothing the chaplain could do to stop what was going on, so he just let it run its course. On that day, things spiralled out of control. The girls who received the Holy Spirit and spoke in tongues could not revert to the language of men, whether English or their local dialect, upon returning to their respectful dormitories. The news eventually reached the head teacher who summoned Patrice to his office and ordered her never again to pray in the school grounds and even threatened to expel her if she did not stop because, according to him, she was causing confusion in the school and disrupting learning.

This is a good example of a similar experience that the disciples of Jesus had which recorded in Acts 4:40:

> "[40] His speech persuaded them. They called the
> apostles in and had them flogged. Then they
> ordered them not to speak in the name of
> Jesus, and let them go."
> Acts 4:40 (NIV)

I cannot remember how the school resolved the issue, but all I know is that scripture union meetings continued. More and more girls accepted Jesus as their Lord and saviour. The entire school atmosphere changed. Most of the girls in the school realized lifestyles of sin according to the bible and abandoned those behaviours. People started behaving as though Jesus would come out the next day and they prayed.

I can remember the tone of evening prep time changing. Instead of chit chatting together before and on their way to prep, most girls headed for the chapel, which was left open 24/7 to pray. Even studying for exams lost the top slot on most of the girls' priority list. The switching of priorities meant that instead of spending more time studying for the final year exams, most girls spent their time praying to God as if Jesus was coming back that year. The interesting thing is that even though I came from a Christian family where attending church was the central part of the family's lifestyle, I did not realise that I was a sinner or that I needed to be saved. I thought that being born of Christian parents and attending church services and even singing in the choir was enough.

Little did I know that true salvation begins with a recognition that all, including me, a daughter of a preacher, have sinned and have come short of the glory of God. In my ignorance, I thought I was okay, and that I was on my way to heaven, until one day, the anointed girl, my best friend Catherine Mbiiza, now Mrs Dyer, and two or three other girls gathered in Catherine's prefects' room to pray.

I did not feel like it that evening and so I felt frustrated that these girls were worshipping and praying when I wanted to sleep. That was a rude awakening for me. I suddenly become uncontrollably violent, waved my arms around and wriggled my whole body. At that point, all the girls surrounded me and started commanding any unclean spirits to get out of me, in Jesus' name. Shortly afterwards, I felt this calm come upon me as if something had left my body and the heaviness I have lived with since my father's death and other unhealthy emotions left me. God delivered me that night.

I wish I could say that from that day on; I started enjoying victorious Christian living, but that is not the case. It was the beginning of trials and temptations of a different kind that demanded my total dependency on God and the support of other believers.

What followed my remarkable conversion was that I became a lover of God and an effective witness of Jesus Christ having become a right-hand girl for the anointed girl by default so that when she got a speaking invitation to other schools, to tell students about Jesus, I would accompany her. I can recall accompanying her when she got an invitation to speak at Choma Secondary school, a mixed school in the same town as our school. Before bringing her message, she asked me up to the podium to accompany her as she sang a rendition of something like; 'You may think it's foolish what I'm going to say.' We did much more together and grew closer and closer as we shared the love of Christ with other girls in our school…

It's amazing how closely people monitor the movement of anyone that becomes a Christian like I did in how it happened to me, although this should surprise no one. Both non-Christians and born-again Christians are good at analysing the life of any Christian whose conversion occurs extraordinarily like mine. No one is immune to this. Even Paul in the bible has critics and those who doubted his salvation because of his past. The story written in Acts 9:26 is about how other believers rejected Paul's testimony by not believing he had really met Jesus.

"[26] When he came to Jerusalem, he tried to join the disciples, but they were all afraid of him, not believing that he really was a disciple." Acts 9:26 (NIV)

The above account of Paul's experience of being rejected by other believers shows everyone needs the support of other believers. Had Barnabas not stood by Paul to defend him and authenticate his testimony of Jesus, appearing to him, who knew what would have become of Paul or even what course his life would have taken? The believers who accepted him based on Barnaba's testimony may not have come to his rescue later, when the Hellenistic Jews planned to kill him. The lesson to be learned here is that when new believers join our churches and communities, we need to welcome them no matter how bad their past is, maybe knowing that they need our love, patience and support as they start their new life as Christians. There is a serious warning in the bible against not warning the sinner, which is tantamount to welcoming newly converted Christians. This is what it says:

"17. Son of man, I have made you a watchman for the house of Israel. Whenever you hear a word from My mouth, give them a warning from Me. 18. If I say to the wicked man, 'You will surely die,' but you do not warn him or speak out to warn him from his wicked way to save his life, that wicked man will die in his iniquity, and I will hold you responsible for his blood." (Ezekiel 3:18)

All this shows is how the world will be at a total loss if believers do not obey God's command to tell others about Jesus and the reason for His death, which was to save humanity from their sins and give them an everlasting life. What is scary in the verse above is the last bit that says that if you do not warn the unbeliever to forsake his wicked ways, the unbeliever will die, and God says He will hold the believer responsible for the unbeliever's blood. I wonder how many believers have read this verse and I wonder how many see the grave consequences of not warning sinners to turn from their wicked ways. I would not be telling the truth if I claimed that I always tell unbelievers about Jesus and warn them of the eternal death that is coming ahead to anyone who refuses to accept salvation that is found in no other than Jesus Christ. In the book of Acts 4:12, the bible says:

> "Salvation is found in no one else, for there
> is no other name under heaven given to
> mankind by which we must be saved."
> (Acts 4:12)

I left Njase in one of the army trucks that arrived at our school to take school leavers on the last day of their exam straight to Kamitonte National Service Camp where we were due to undertake rigorous military training to prepare for the war that was imminent between my country (home country) and a neighbouring country which was at the time still under white rule. I remember the hype that filled the air as these enormous trucks arrived to pick up all the school leavers for youth service. There was a mixture of excitement and apprehension, not knowing what youth service had for us, but adrenaline kept us going. Everyone felt safe in each other's company and sang our hearts out as the huge vehicles sped away from the charged scene outside the school reception under the watch of remaining students and the teachers.

There were tears of joy at the prospect of completing Form Five but deep-seated feelings of apprehension at the thought of heading away from freedom to start life in restricted army barracks where we were going to train as back up soldiers at a camp far away from the rest of the community; where green combat uniforms that composed of a pair of trousers, a long-sleeved shirt, a pair of black boots, a pair of socks and a green Barret to complete the set awaited our arrival. In hindsight, I don't know what that was all about. We were all subjected to intense endurance training for the entire year and I mean severe training; digging trenches, walking with rucksacks and rifles on our backs with very little to eat and drink.

I can remember going to bed at night one evening just to wake up to a command to form up, as the command wanted everyone to convene in a designated place. It was the custom of the youth camp to keep trainees in suspense of the night for embarking on the next level of training which involved being woken up in the early hours of the morning without warning of being expected to get dressed up in full combat within the time allocated, which was something ridiculously small, like five to ten minutes for you to get dressed and present yourself at the designated spot within that time.

Youth service was a challenging time but there were many benefits to be gained for those who attended and managed to 'fall in', the term used at the start of an activity by the time they 'fell out', the term used at the end. There were two levels of training. The first which was known as the trainee phase, which was for beginners and the 'pass out phase' which was for those about to leave youth service.

What I loved about being at youth service was Christian union gatherings. The meetings that took place for youth camp were of a different calibre to those that took place elsewhere. There was a seriousness in which people engaged at these meetings and I had seen nowhere else. I can only compare those meetings to the Njase experience when the anointed girl first came. No one joked or took praying at youth camp lightly.

I remember snapping at a couple of girls when I overheard them using obscene language at the court while waiting to form up. My spirit was so in tune with God as sensitive to the Holy Spirit that I felt uncomfortable when I heard anyone saying or doing anything that was not pleasing to God.

I remember saying to this couple; 'How can you talk like that? Don't you know it is a sin and an offence to God?'

Strangely, they did not react or respond to me, but just remained silent. I can only imagine that God's presence was with me and it must have been the Holy Spirit that made me open my mouth and the courage to say what I said to them. Writing this into account makes me wonder where I am spiritually at present. Have I not undergone spiritual growth at the right rate, which means I am not where I should be in my walk with God? Or am I okay and therefore there's no need to worry? May God help me.

The question I asked in the preceding paragraph is one every believer should ask themselves. This is so because they say that backsliding is not just the retrogression a believer might experience in their walk with God, a state of lagging the normal growth rate a believer undergoes from the time of becoming a Christian to where they examine themselves. All I can say is that I know what has happened to me and I know what I need to do to return to my first love and recharge the anointing I enjoyed when I first got saved.

The last phase of living with my mum was when I worked for a national bank as a teller. My life changed for the better almost overnight. I started earning a decent wage from the bank that was more than sufficient for my whole family. I enjoyed taking care of my mother and living with my sister Elizabeth in a large house which used to belong to a man called Mitimingi, a quiet man. He at one stage tried to ask my hand in marriage without first going into courtship and as he was not a believer, I turned his proposal down and I think that was when we moved from his house live in a Mr Mutiya's house which was near the road leading to the nearby village.

Mr Mutiya's house must have had about seven bedrooms as it could accommodate my sister Eliya, her husband and my sister Elizabeth, who at this point on separation from her first husband, the father of her first three children.

Spending time with my two sisters and my mum was something special. Mum was a prayer warrior who prayed the night out and prayed the day in. She never stopped mentioning my dad throughout her life. She always recalled his preaching and his love for God, even in suffering until his death at 47 in 1969.

Chapter 3

A Taste of Love and Luxury When I Lived with My Brother Jonas and His Family

Once I left my mum in January 1979, I did not return to live with her again until 1981, when I had my first son, Danny. I spent the rest of my secondary school years at boarding school during the term or with my brother John and his family, first in Livingstone and later in Lusaka, before they moved to the Copperbelt, where they remained until his death in 1994.

The phase of my life living with John and his family was very special. Both John and his wife Austria loved me as if I was one of their own children. I had such a wonderful life with them. I almost forgot the pain of losing my dad for a while. John, ten or more years older than me, became the father that I never had. He paid my school fees and supplied whatever I needed for my education. They opened their home to me and made me feel at home.

There was something about living with John and Austria. They gave me a proper sense of belonging and were very protective of me. They allowed no other family to get in between us. That is just what I needed for my healing, to feel protected and safe. I loved their children Nalituba, Rekha, and their late brother Mudenda, with whom I bonded with a very special bond. I can remember teaching the girls the nursery rhymes while having a great aunty—niece's time with them in the evenings before bed, singing:

"Christopher Columbus was a great man; he flew to America in a flying pan; the weather went higher, and higher, and over."

Their home became my base during school holidays from when I was in form two till I completed my form five of my secondary school. They lived in an affluent area of Livingstone, called 217. I can remember going out with my sister-in-law to the market sometimes just for a walk and at other times for a bit of top-up shopping since they normally bought everything in bulk and so they needed a car to do the normal grocery shopping. I can also remember a vegetable garden which was in front of the house where the worker used to grow green vegetables, cucumbers, carrots and tomatoes. So, we used to eat fresh vegetables straight from the family vegetable garden.

An incident involving a tall Lozi boy comes to mind at this point. Remember, I was a Christian girl and going with boys was taboo, not only for me as a born again and godly girl, but for the entire community. I had developed personal Christian values that made me decide I would do nothing that would be an offence to God and disrespectful to my brother and his wife. On this occasion, I went out with Rebecca to visit an older school mate from Njase, who was a very close friend.

On our way back, we bumped into a boy I had met during our train trips back to school, as he was a student of St Marks Boys Secondary School somewhere in the south. He was one of the many boys who had a crush on me and kept following me whenever he saw me. On this occasion, he may have touched my hand; I felt uneasy, pulled my hand away and swerved when he tried kissing my chick. That was a big sin in those days and it still is in Christian circles. I never thought much of it until at the dinner table when Rekha blurted out from nowhere, 'Aunty Sophie, who was that boy that tried to kiss you?' May God forgive me for lying when my brother stopped eating and demanded an explanation. It was the first time I had seen my brother so angry. I quickly made up a girl's name and said, 'That was my friend Molly; ' which was obviously not his real name. Then my brother's anger subsided. I now want to ask every reader's forgiveness for not telling my brother the truth. I know God forgave me a long time ago when I asked Him to.

That became one of the saddest days during my time with the Chifuwe's. I told a lie to cover up because I was afraid of what my brother would have done to me. Looking back from where I am as a mature Christian, I think I should have explained exactly what had happened, hard as it may have been. That nearly spoiled the good relationships that we always shared in that house. Before the incident, I only knew love and affirmation from my brother and his family. They affirmed and gave me all the support I could have asked for, so I did not expect the anger my brother showed and could not take it. Unfortunately for me, my sister-in-law was not home on that day. The next thing I did was to remove myself from the lounger where everyone was and going to lie down in my bedroom in broad daylight. Then suddenly, sensed an unusual darkness come over me. That scared me. I was so afraid that i got up and went back to the lounge where my brother was watching television with his girls and joined them. To this day, I do not know what that was about, but I suspect it was the spirit of depression that was about to set in. I knew I could not accept it, so I refused to stay in that room alone for fear that if I did, I may have sunk deeper and deeper into depression. That was why I made the tough decision to return to the very place where the very person who had upset me was.

Why am I writing about an incident with a boy? It's for showing readers that whether one is undergoing bereavement, people around you see you for who you are outside, and it's down to you to live as normally as possible. Also, I am trying to be real to myself and show others that even Christian girls are attractive to non-Christian boys and even more so. Remember, I was growing up as a girl without a father and therefore so, although my brother did a good job of playing dad to me, I still missed the love of our father and so I had a level of vulnerability around men. My father was a loving and supportive father and so the gap he left when he died was too big to be filled easily.

When I look back, I can see God even in this incident. He must have been watching over me and so gave me the strength to reject the spirit of depression and thankfully, it disappeared immediately, and I never felt it ever again. This is what they call grace. I did not pray, or ask anyone to pray for me, but I took the right decision and overcome depression in an instant. No wonder my husband Molland always reminds me not to boast about the gift of prayer and faith that the Lord has given me, but to remember that He has given it to me not because I deserve it, but because of His grace. He keeps reminding me how blessed I am that being how I have survived so many tough situations in my life. That I never sank into depression the day I just described is just one of the many miracles God has performed in my life.

Attending church was the highlight of living with the Chifuwes even though they were not Pentecostals like I was. They were Adventists. Although I attended the Seventh Day Adventist Church with them when they moved from Livingstone. It was when my brother got a better job with a private company called Lusaka Opticians, and the job came with transport and a beautiful three-bedroom house with an annex in a much sought after but expensive area of Makeni. I can remember us enjoying recreational activities like table tennis, which we used to play at home when we were not going out. I used to enjoy going to places like botanical gardens in Lusaka to see animals and just spend a day out as a family.

Something funny happened once when we visited a Mundawanga botanical garden based in a place a few miles away from Lusaka that I will never forget. My nieces Nalituba and Rekha got so fascinated with the pink bottoms of the monkeys. They couldn't stop making funny comments and pointing at the poor monkeys. I cannot remember their exact comments, but I know their comments made be laughing so hard that my chest hurt.

A sad incident while living with the Chifuwes was when we had a robbery in the Makeni home while we had an elderly couple, Paul and Lucy Golf, visiting with us. I was fast asleep in my bedroom with the girls when I heard loud noises, just realise there had been a break in. When I think about it now, the robbery was a planned because when the robbers knocked on my brother's bedroom window; they called him by name. My sister-in-law tried to stop my brother from opening the door, as she suspected that it may have been a setup, even if they were calling his name. My brother, who knew so many people, ignored her warning and went and opened the door just to find a group of men standing outside the door at gunpoint. They immediately demanded to be taken to his guest room.

Not knowing what else to do, my brother led the men to the bedroom where Lucy and Peter were sleeping. Upon entering, they commanded my brother to leave the room with one robber at gunpoint who asked him to lead the way to his bedroom where they demanded money, jewellery and other precious things. But before they got to the bedroom, my sister-in-law devised a brilliant idea to make it difficult for the robbers to see what was in their bedroom. So, she removed the light bulbs from the holders to make the bedroom dark.

While this was going on in the main house, something else was going on in the annex. The robbers seemed to have worked out that there was another visitor, whose name I cannot remember, who was visiting my brother from Uganda at the same time as the Golfs. So, the robbers broke into the annex and bound both Chiseya and my brother's guest and left them. Once the robber assigned to watch the people in the annex had tied them to their beds, he went outside and started eating mangos from the tree at the back of my brother's house. At that point, Chiseya quietly loosened himself despite the repeated pleas by the guest to stop for fear that if the robber returned and found him trying to escape, he may have shot them. After untying himself, Chiseya ran to the house of a neighbour who was an ex-soldier to get help. To his surprise, neither the ex-soldier nor his younger brother would help.

At that point, Chiseya devised his own rescue plan to help my brother. He took a large pole on his way from that neighbour's house and quietly crept to the man who was eating mangoes and, with a loud shout, hit him with the pole. The man shouted out to his friends and they all run off, but by this time, they had already removed several items from my brother's house to a van that was waiting a few yards away. Prior to Chiseya scaring the man off, my brother, for whatever reason, had told the man who was harassing him for money that he had given some money to his young sister, who was asleep in the bedroom opposite him. The man then came, stood outside our bedroom and demanded that I open the door. I was shaking so much that I could not even put the key in the hole. The man kept shouting and threatening to break the door open, but the more he shouted, the more I shook.

Just as I had inserted the key into the hole and unlocked the door, a warning shout from the man who Chiseya had struck came and off the man went, even before setting his eyes on me and the girls or us on him. There are many other interesting incidents I could share about my life with the Clifton's, but this book shows the reader that there's nothing insurmountable in life. Sadly, my brother never recovered the stolen things, and the local police failed to bring the men to justice, even though a rumour saying the police knew who they were was circulating. How sad is that? No wonder the bible warns us in the ninth verse of Psalms 118, which says,

"It is better to take refuge in the LORD than to trust in humans." (Psalm 118:9)

The above verse is so true, especially during modern days when lawlessness is on the rise. It seems as if law enforcement departments are losing the plot. The police have lost the ability to maintain order and security for the safety of the people of the nations.

As my life with the Clifton's was great, with no cause to worry because I had enough to eat, drink and to put on, this phase of my life did not sit well with the purpose of this book. I wrote this book to use it as an opportunity to share the impact that grief had on me and how putting my faith in God brought me healing and gave me a cause to carry on with my life and get over the pain and trauma I went through in my early days. My life with this family was my first taste of luxury. It was the beginning of my recovery. My brother and his wife even used to attend my sports days and other events to make me feel like a normal girl receiving parental love.

I see God's love and care for me through my relationship with him and his wife. God must have orchestrated my stay with them so that I could start my journey of healing. I started feeling normal again and regained my self-esteem and confidence from the support I received from this family. No words of thanks can repay them for what they did for me, just like I told my niece Lucy Redmond when she attended my daughter's wedding in November 2016.

The love John and his wife Austria showed me is the reason I look at their children like my actual family, which they are. They helped me to forget my sorrows to a certain extent, although since I never got my father or my siblings back, my healing is not yet complete because although the inner pain and sorrow are nothing compared to the many good times I have had and the strong family bonds I formed with the Chifuwes.

I have had moments, especially when my peace gets interrupted by something or the atmosphere I am in is not right for me when I still struggle. However, if sad memories try to surface, I have learned to stand on bible promises to resist them and stay in control. My half sister Mary Mudenda played quite an important role in my life when I was at the National Service in a north western village of my country. Her home became the base for me to stop on my way to and from the camp. My brother John would put me on the coach and ask my sister Mary and husband Simons to meet me at the other end and take me to theirs. An incident happened once when I stopped over at the Mudendas. An insect got into my ear as it was a rainy season and lots of insects fly around during the rainy season.

Unfortunately for me, there was a curfew in the city where they lived, and I cannot remember what the curfew was about. It may have been the time when a murderer was on the loose and the police wanted everyone indoors between the hours of 08:00 in the morning and 20:00 in the evening, if my memory serves me right. As time passed, the pain in my ear grew worse, possibly because the insect which was still alive was going the wrong way while trying to get out. My sister- and brother-in-law had no option but to break the curfew law and drive me to the general hospital. By this time, I had lost consciousness.

In hindsight, I can see how I could have potentially lost my life had they not taken a risk of driving me to the hospital. In fact, I read a few stories during the writing of this book about two children and a man who lost their lives because an insect had entered through their ears and crawled to the brain where they remained alive. That makes me even more thankful to God for sparing my life, to my sister and her husband for taking me to the hospital. The hospital team removed the insect from my ear, although I cannot remember how they did it as I was in a comma. Strangely, I still continued pulling insect's body parts from my ear many years later. For instance, once while cleaning my ears when I was at the Natural Resources Development College, I pulled out insect's leg mixed with ear wax.

I spent time with another step sister Elina, while she lived with my brother John following her divorce. Interesting things I don't wish to go into happened. Aside from that, I used to feel comfortable with her as an elder sister. I remember her trying to get me into a job where she worked. Although this did not work in the end, I still owe her many thanks for her effort. As my elder sister, she used to do all elder sister favours, which I used to enjoy, like pass a nice skirt over or share some face cream and makeup.

My other step brother Aaron Chifuwe took my sister Elizabeth in and put her in a school near him. He kept in touch and checked on everyone whenever he could, many years later. He helped to move my nephew Charles from Lusaka, where he lived with his father, and stepfamily to Kitwe to live with my late sister Elizabeth close to my mum, who lived in the same yard with my sister.

With love, encouragement and support from my sister Elizabeth and my mum, Charles completed his secondary school with excellent results. He continued living with my sister until her demise in 2014. Although things got tough for him following my sister's demise, he was a grown man and so he could make ends meet for himself with my sister's children, his cousins' support. I had to learn to let God take control, otherwise I may have made myself worried sick wondering what he had eaten, where he was and what was happening to him.

I have nothing but thanks for my stepbrothers and sisters. They have always been there for us, even though it hasn't always been easy. Our family has not been immune to family feuds and fights, but overall, we have been there for each other when it mattered the most.

Chapter 4

Student of the Natural Resources Development College

Loss and bereavement do not excuse anyone from doing the things of life necessary to lead a normal and decent life. This includes going to school, going to college, and getting a job. While I felt broken inside, but never expressed it, I still needed to gain a qualification to better myself and increase my chances of living a happy life, not because of a job, but because of growing in my social intelligence. Every person should try going to a college or another institution of learning because campus life is unlike anything else. Everything happens there, and that's where one's true colours come out. My goal was to embark on a fulfilling career, so college was the beginning.

I joined the college of agriculture in 1981 to do an agricultural course, just because agricultural science was one of my favourite subjects at school. My brother Jonas was instrumental in me getting into college when I couldn't get directly into the university to do medicine, which was my first choice because my mathematics results let me down despite being one of the top mathematics students at school.

Broken as I was inside, it never showed outwardly. I can remember being taken to my class and making people think I was a junior lecturer when I sat in the front roll. So, during introductions, I said my name, but still people took me as a lecturer just because the boys felt that my entire presentation and personality did not suit agricultural science, which involved handling mess from animals and from plants. In fact, one of my classmates spoke out and said, 'What does she want in this class? She can't be an agricultural science student, surely looking like this. She's in a wrong career.' Anyway, the rest is history. I stayed not only for that day but for three years until I graduated and gained my qualification.

My experience in this case is an example of how people can find it easy to label other people wrongly by jumping to conclusions and not bothering to find out what might go on and why. Had I not remained and do the course, I wanted to become an agricultural scientist and not a nutritionist, as with 90% of the girls who came to study at college. I could have listened to other students, and had I started feeling out of place and exited the college out of frustration that could have led me to making an unplanned career change and abandonment of the career of my choice.

In the bible, a story is told of how God sent the prophet Samuel to anoint David to be king but when he saw David's brother's stature, he thought it was him God had sent to anoint, until the Lord stopped him and told him not to be deceived by the way Simeon looked.

"[7] But the Lord said to Samuel, 'Do not consider
his appearance or his height, for I have
rejected him. The Lord does not look at the

things people look at. People look at the outward
appearance, but the Lord looks at the heart.'"
(I Samuel 16:7)

I joined the college's scripture union and attended prayer meetings in the mornings once a week and fellowship meetings every Friday and met many wonderful Christian men and women. We were closely knit as Christians and got to know each other well. I remember suffering with a phobia that made me fear sleeping on my own. It was such a dark and heavy spirit. I even had to sleep in my opposite door neighbours' room, another Christian girl, until one day, God delivered me. I remember this incident like it happened yesterday. It was the first day of the term and so everyone was arriving back at college, having spent time away on holiday. I remember two brothers coming to see me to find out how I was and whether I still had the phobia to which I said yes. They read the verse in the bible found in 1 John 3:8, which says:

"8. The one who does what is sinful is of the devil, because the devil has been sinning from the beginning. The reason the Son of God appeared was to destroy the devil's work." (1 John 3:8)

Then they prayed for me, and I got delivered instantly. This is one of the many experiences I have had about praying using the word of God. I cannot overemphasise the fact that the bible is the word of God and as it says in the book of Isaiah 55:10–11 which says,

"Just as rain does not fall and not help plants to grow, everything God says also comes to pass." (Isaiah 55:10–11)

Something beautiful happened while I was at college. It's something I have never forgotten. It was during my college years that I received a letter from my brother John in which he had put the verse from Jeremiah 29:11 and expanded on it. I remember feeling a sense of reassurance when I read this verse that almost wrote my destiny, because the verse jumped out to me and gave me hope for the future. The verse says;

"[11] *'For I know the plans I have for you,' declares the Lord,*
'plans to prosper you and not to harm you,
plans to give you hope and a future.'"
(Jeremiah 29:11)

God prompted my brother to write to me and include the verse in the letter because he was not in the habit of sharing scriptures with me. I in fact, do not remember one occasion when he said anything from the word of God to me the whole time I had lived with him. If spoken in faith, the word of God can change things for the benefit of those who use it and for God's glory. My time at the college of agriculture was a mixture of sadness and bliss because I had not yet discovered the true me.

It took me some time to become fully healed from the trauma of losing so many family members, especially my father, even though I have never shared the sorrow I felt with anyone. I grew from strength to strength thanks to the love and acceptance of my mother, my brother and his family, my sisters, and the friends I made along the way. Fellowship with other Christians has been the highlight of my life. It was a joy to attend Christian union and church meetings and sing hymns and choruses that spoke directly to me.

I remember a special experience I had one Sunday morning while attending church at the Northmead Assemblies of God church in Lusaka, Zambia, in 1982. A visiting minister from South Africa who brought his choir along to sing during the crusade, the church invited him as guest speaker called people out for prayer. I desperately wanted prayer and so I went forward. I cannot remember what happened, but suddenly, I heard this loud scream come out of me before I passed out. The next thing I knew is that I was in the vestibule with several people praying for me. When I came around, they asked me how I was, and I told them I was fine. Although I was aware of where I was, but I could not work out how I ended up in the vestibule.

This incident made some members of the scripture union question my salvation. I can remember many speculation going on within the group. Some even suspected demon possession, while others wondered whether I was a genuine believer. This here is an example of unacceptable conduct which is displayed amongst Christians. It is a failure by members of the body of Christ to show their new nature when it matters most. As a result, it has the potential to discourage young believers and drive away unbelievers. This is a sad and unhealthy state of affairs that no one expects to see in Christian circles. According to James 4: 11, here is what the bible says about judging others:

"11. Brothers and sisters, do not slander one another. Anyone who speaks against a brother or sister or judges them speaks against the law and judges it. When you judge the law, you are not keeping it, but sitting in judgment on it." (James 4:11)

The reaction I got from other Christians following what happened to me at the assemblies of God church does not surprise me because even Jesus went through it. His own disciples questioned his every move, despite being the closest to him. The Pharisees and Sadducees were even worse. They did not believe that He was the son of God and even called him names. A good example is the account of Jesus healing a man on the Sabbath found in Mark 3:2, which says:

"2 And they watched Jesus,[a] to see whether he would heal him on the Sabbath, so that they might accuse him. 3" (Mark 3:2)

There is something about religious people who focus on dos and don'ts. They seem to be bent on trying to follow man made regulations even when God has the final say to every matter and He wants to show them a different way. They don't seem to understand that souls of men come first to God because He does not wish that any should perish. God sent Jesus into the world only for one purpose; to save and seek the lost not because they obey the law, but because they accept His love. God, in His mercy, has been helping sinners to understand that God loves them the way they are, and He will forgive their sins if they ask Him. This is the reason God does not want Christians to go around condemning people because of their sins. He rather wants them to show His loving and forgiving nature to everyone, especially those that are still lost in sin.

Those members of the college scripture union who judged me when I passed out during a powerful meeting and then hands laid on me for prayer did so because they were not in God's will. Otherwise, they would have sought to find out from me what had happened so they could pray for me. A story is told in the book of Acts in the bible about Paul, when islanders suspected him of being a murderer when a snake wound itself on his hand in Malta. Here is it just in case you do not have a bible and to save you from having to find it:

"4 When the islanders saw the snake hanging from his hand, they said to each other, 'This man must be a murderer; for though he escaped from the sea, the goddess Justice has not allowed him to live.' 5 But Paul shook the snake off into the fire and suffered no ill effects." (Act 28:4–5)

I have included this story here just to show the reader that when people judge you wrongly, do not despair. Give them a chance to find out the truth and change their mind. Do not vindicate yourself. Just keep doing the right thing until the truth comes out and watches them turn around. Do not even disown them or separate yourself from them because if you do that, they will never know that you were innocent and, therefore, will continue believing their lies and this is not good for them or for you.

Chapter 5

Things All Christian Girls Should Be Aware of When They First Go to College

I also want to share my experience as a young, naïve and timid teenage girl at college being away from my family for the first time. I remember the horrible experience I had the very first night I spent alone in a college hall of residence. It was hard for me to deal with the behaviour of boys knocking on my door after ten o'clock demanding to come in. I remember shaking to the core with fear behind my locked door, wondering what would happen to me if the door suddenly zoomed open. Luckily, the house keeper rescued me. Her job was to supervise the girls' hostels, especially during fresher's week when new, young and naive girls arrive. She must have known that some girls like me might need her help from her experience of the boy's behaviour during fresher's week. After all, she had been in post for several years, and therefore suspected that the likes of me might need her help that night.

That night, she was patrolling the girls' hostess and then came to mine. She seemed to hang around the first floor where my room was situated for a while until the boys started turning up one by one like vultures looking for prey. She tried to drive them away one by one but as soon as one left, another one came until she knew she was fighting a losing battle and took me with her, so I could spend the night in one of the empty rooms next to her flat. In hindsight, I felt cross that I let myself down just because of a lack of experience in dealing with boys and this was partly because I attended a girl's only secondary school and so had no prior exposure to the behaviour of boys towards girls.

My first term at college was horrible. I hated the boys paying me too much unwanted attention all the time. I was the only girl in my class of about thirty agricultural science students did not help. It always made me feel good when I went for the combined Agricultural Business Management lessons where I would meet up with another student, the only other woman in the agricultural science department, and to crown it all, she was also a Christian. I remember hating lunch times. We had to walk to the dining hall from our various classes. It was a dreadful walk so much that I occasionally almost missed my lunch, but for my best friend, who would make sure I made the walk to the dining hall with her on days her classes finished at the same time as mine. All the naughty boys used to fight to sit along the aisles leading to the food counters during meals just to see the girls walk in and start the stupid boys whistling and hissing, although the college did not condone such within the college grounds. I feel embarrassed to even allude to some reasons the boys used to line up along the dining hall isles but all I can say is that boys are boys and only strong girls brought up with Christian values and good morals can safely escape the bait the devil uses these boys to catch innocent girls.

I felt a powerful urge to include my experiences with boys to warn any young woman who may one day find themselves in a university hall of residence or a shared house away from the radar of their parents and other family members to take care of themselves. Without personal values and enough courage to stand up to these boys, you must show them that girls are not just sex symbols or objects for boys to play with as and when. They have values, their bodies are precious and therefore they will not let any wild and weird boys to take advantage of them. This is where belonging to a Christian union group comes handy. It's more likely that scrupulous men take advantage of young women and pressure them to succumb to immoral activities that go on in institutions of higher learning if they are not answerable to a group or an older person, bearing in mind their parents are not there.

In my case, I had already formed strong-personal values, and I was fully aware of what lifestyles not to embark on just because I was away from my family. However, I went through a mixture of emotions that fluctuated from feelings of sadness and apprehension now and again, as my healing was not yet complete. I also felt optimistic and expected a good job and a better God-ordained future after graduating as an agricultural science specialist. I looked forward to living somewhere in a safe and peaceful part of the country. Settling in a good Pentecostal church was always on the top of my priority list. The question to ask is; did I, as a Christian girl, have the parable of the rich fool told by Jesus in the bible at the back of my mind?

In the story, which is found in the book of Luke chapter 12 from verse 18 to 20, we learn that this man had big plans for his future. He wanted to expand his barns to store more of his harvest, thinking he would be secure for the rest of his life until Jesus made him realise he had no control over his life and gathering much wealth guarantees no one a long secure life.

Another key question to ask is; how many successful people are there in our world today who totally disregard the existence of God and carry on as if the wealth they amass can prevent them from dying from cancer, dementia, heart disease, AIDS, sugar diabetes and many more incurable diseases? No one can dispute the benefits of advanced but costly medical services can give those who can afford them but ultimately, the rich and the poor, the famous and the obscure, the black, white, yellow and brown all experience the same symptoms from the same diseases and die in the same way. In Mark 8:36, the bible says;

"^{36} For what shall it profit a man, if he shall gain the whole world, and lose his own soul?" (Mark 8:36)

What a sobering question? Would it not be great if everyone realised the implications this verse has on their vocational commitments and the priorities they make in life? Even King Solomon, the richest man there ever was said in Ecclesiastes 1:2–3:

"^{2} 'Meaningless! Meaningless!'
says the Teacher. 'Utterly meaningless!
Everything is meaningless.'
^{3} What do people gain from all their labours
at which they toil under the sun?" (Ecclesiastes 1:1–3)

For anyone whose main aim in life is to gather as much wealth as they might manage, answer the question asked by king Solomon in the bible quote above: what will I gain from toiling day and night and being denied time to rest and be with my family, for those that have families? Any commitments that stop a man or woman from spending quality time with their families need questioning and every effort made to factor in family and friend's time in your daily life.

Many a rich man has learned the vital lesson of never neglecting their families as in they risk losing them in the long run and many have confessed regretting in putting their vocational activities before their families and some have sadly lost their families and their joy with them and have lived the most miserable lives till their dying day.

The Entrepreneur Europe magazine has listed five areas that no one should ever sacrifice for work. At the top of their list sits health, followed by family, interest or hobbies, relationships and lastly integrity. In all honesty, I do not completely agree with the order in which they have listed the areas because if I wrote them, I would have put integrity at the top, followed by family and the other three could have sat in any position.

It's great to see that relationships and hobbies are on the list of the five important things never to be neglected for work because, as the saying goes, 'Work alone and no play makes Jack a dull boy.' There was a time in my life when I could not stomach this saying because I did not accept that play had to be a part of work. To me, work mattered more than play, and so it was okay to work and work, even if there was no time to play. I saw play as something that needed to be thought about only if there was time to spare. I have learned over the years that if that was the case, some people would have no time to relax or for recreational activities, which are equally important.

God has blessed because, as an athlete and a long-distance runner representing my institutions during my school days, I developed a desire for engaging in recreational activities by default. This helped me to develop a special way of settling back into study mood after getting interrupted during term time to travel for games representing my school. I left my school so many times during term and travelled to other towns for sports. I was the 8000 and 15000 meter runner and my school and provincial champion. It became a part of my term time calendar and thankfully it never affected my performance in my academic work as I continued achieving good grades in my exams.

It is important to understand that one who is born a Christian and the fact that one is born from Christian parents who make you go to church in obedience to them does not make one a Christian either.

Chapter 6

God Saved Me from AIDS a Hundred Times Over

After I graduated from the college of agriculture, I joined the Ministry of Agriculture and Fisheries, as the government called the ministry then. My first placement was in a small town called Choma in Zambia. Prior to my graduation, I had heard about the rural tours all employees of the ministry of agriculture had to undertake in order to monitor animal and crop production in rural areas. District and Block Agricultural Officers supervised farmers' activities in the absence of Provincial Specialist Officers. I thought little of the tours until I started working full time for the ministry.

To ensure that farmers were following correct and safe farming methods, the district and block agricultural officers worked closely with each individual farmer and would visit them daily. The provincial specialist officers travelled at least once a month to visit the district and block officers for training, and to drop seeds, equipment and run workshops. We would spend five nights away from home. Working in this way kept me busy and seemed to drown my grief, at least to a certain extent. However, this meant that I travelled in the company of men all the time, as I was one of the few women operating from the provincial headquarters of the ministry.

When I first graduated, I was single and lived with my mum. This was a good idea, as everyone knew and respected that. However, my experience of travelling with only men one week in a month was not a pleasant one. When I say that most of the men I travelled with attempted to come into my room during the night when they had returned from a drinking evening after the day's work with the farmers, I just do not understand men's behaviour. Most of them do not have any sense of danger or any restraint. It was so sad to see so many of my colleagues come back from pubs with women that they had met at the pub and openly take them into their hotel rooms until the next day. As a Christina woman, that was so heart-breaking and frustrating to watch and made me not enjoy my job the next day as I did not feel like talking to any of them anymore. Believe it or, they carried on as normal the next day.

The sad part of this story is that as I am writing this book now, many of these men are under six feet as they contracted 'Acquired Immune Deficiency Syndrome' or AIDS, which was rampant. How my colleagues could do what they did during those terrible AIDS days leaves me speechless. I know this sounds naïve, but what is wrong with men? I could not understand why they failed to learn from so many of their friends and families that had paid the price of similar behaviours? To this day, I can remember some of them saying daft things like joking about it the next day. They used to say things like, If I get AIDS, then so be it etc. These are men that in most cases had wives and children. The way they carried on made me wonder why their wives and children mattered less when they were out of sight, at least going by their ill-disciplined behaviours. The pleasure of one week made them lose their senses and made them do shameful things. This goes a long way to prove that the bible says in Jeremiah 17 verse 9; that,

"The heart is deceitful above all things and
desperately wicked; who can know it?" (Jeremiah 17:9)

Writing this section of my book is the least comfortable task, but I have to write it to warn the reader. Had I not had the Christian values that were instilled in me both at home and at my Christian school, I would never have survived the AIDS that most of my colleagues had because I could open my door when my colleagues knocked, hoping to come in. If I did, I could have contracted AIDS as well and would be dead by now. I write this to thank God for preserving my life. For protecting the families of the male colleagues implied in this story, I will not list them, but I am sad to say that it was almost every male colleague that I travelled with and I later learned that some of them planned trips just to take me out so that they could get into my room during the night but thankfully, that was not my lifestyle.

As a born again Christian, with a reverential fear of God, and because of my godly upbringing, I did not get involved in what they thought was fun and that protected me from AIDS and from losing my Christian identity compromising with my values. Because I exercised great self-control and decided not to entertain attempts by these men to get into my bedroom, I am still alive today. I felt cross throughout the week when this happened and refused to spend any time with any of the men until, to the glory of God, word started going around that I was different and there was no use taking me on a tour as no one had succeeded to convince me to sin with me. What a sad world we live in. It is a fallen world, full of men and women who see nothing wrong with having extra-marital affairs. They don't seem to care how their extra-marital affairs affect their spouses and children.

This has led to the breakdown of morals in society because the number of children growing up in single-parent households and those growing up with no father figures is on the rise and it's no wonder juvenile crime rate is on the increase and no one seems to have an answer to it. It seems as if no one cares and no one is accountable to anyone for anything. There's now a common phrase and I often hear people using this phrase; 'This is me, that's how I want to live my life,' regardless of how their chosen lifestyle affects others around them.

Regrettably, the world is becoming a lawless place where even law enforcement units of nations are failing to control unruly and criminal behaviour. Children as young as eight are being groomed for selling drugs. Lack of self-control and moral degradation has become commonplace, and this has been going on for years. As long as government leaders do not introduce stringent measures for controlling lawless behaviour, things will get worse. The world might become one dangerous crime scene which will cost many lives. From a Christian point of view, what is going on is a sure sign that the end of time is not far off, even though no one knows when this is actually going to be.

If nothing is done to put new laws and more stringent measures for controlling lawless behaviour, the world will become one dangerous crime scene which will cost many lives. From a Christian point view, what is going on is a sure indication that the end of time is not far off even though no one knows when this is actually going to be. Going by what is written in 2 Timothy 2:3;

"3. But mark this: There will be terrible times in the last days. [2] People will be lovers of themselves, lovers of money, boastful, proud, abusive, disobedient to their parents, ungrateful, unholy, [3] without love, unforgiving, slanderous, without self-control, brutal, not lovers of the good, [4] treacherous, rash, conceited, lovers of pleasure rather than lovers of God – [5] having a form of godliness but denying its power. Have nothing to do with such people." (2 Timothy 2:1-5)

Prior to working for the ministry of Agriculture, I worked for a commercial bank and experienced the same pressure from both married and unmarried men. I know that this should not surprise anybody but all the same it's not right. If it costs lives and breaks down families, then it should not be entertained. Just as many died of the dreadful disease of AIDS in the ministry of agriculture, many died of the same in the commercial bank and even there, many attempted to go out with me.

If you are a man and you are reading this book, just think about what carelessness and lack of self-control could cost you. When people fell ill, it was no longer funny and sad that their poor wives had to bear the pressure of looking after them if they themselves did not get infected and after death, taking care of children if they also did not follow. What's the point? Isn't this a good reason for people to find out how to live self-controlled lives and enjoy lives that are satisfied because the void in every man's heart is filled with God? Why don't people try living their lives the Christian way? I am not by any means suggesting that Christian people do not make mistakes, because they do but it's different. In 1 John 2:1, the bible says:

"My dear children, I write this to you so that you will not sin. But if anybody does sin, we have an advocate with the Father, Jesus Christ, the Righteous One."

The good news is that, for everyone who becomes a Christian and starts reading the bible, they discover God's nature and understand that only God can fill the void that so many try to fill with things like alcohol, cigarettes, drugs, sex and money. Paul from the bible wrote these words to the Romans in chapter 12:1:

"12. I beseech you therefore, brethren, by the mercies of God, that ye present your bodies a living sacrifice, holy, acceptable unto God, which is your reasonable service."

I urge anyone who has not yet tried the way of the bible to try it. It's the safest, the most peaceful and enjoyable way of life with the promise of everlasting life with God in Heaven. I have heard many who had a near death life experience testify to the existence of heaven and change their lives after that experience. This may be the only chance that you have to try with the God of the bible. Why don't you speak to a Christian in your circles about God and see how things go for you afterwards?

I believe I survived a lot of situations that could have cost me my life just because of living my life on Christian values. There's nothing to lose and everything to gain.

Chapter 7

Leaving Zambia for the United Kingdom

If anyone told me forty years ago that I was going to get married, have children and not only leave the little suburban town of Zambia but better still immigrate to Great Britain, I would have told them they were out of their mind. Can you imagine being born in a small suburban district of Zambia, spending your early years there and being content with your life? Leaving that sort of place twenty years ago would have been the last thing on one's mind, especially for someone like me who had undergone countless traumatic events, with a young life plagued with so much death within the family.

They say that you do not choose where you are born, but you can choose where you live; and you do not choose your parents, but you can choose how you respond to their negative or positive parenting and choose whether to treat them with respect owing to your judgement of their parenting skills. I certainly did not choose to be born in Kalomo, a small suburban town of Southern Zambia about 340 kilometres from Lusaka, Zambia's capital city, neither did I choose the circumstances I have had to put up with in my life, but I chose not to let them break me down. My adversity has given me reason to strive to become stronger as I continue refusing to be defeated by them.

In her book, 'You Cannot Choose Your Parents, but You Can Choose Your Future,' Helen Woo, possibly a non-Christian, describes her unpleasant memories of being brought up in an Asian country under the Chinese culture. She talks of being a victim of the tiger mother phenomenon as she unveils the story of her tough childhood. Some reviews are not that great. One review has called Helen a crying wolf attacking her own parents and family to make a living. Another one has accused her of being a greedy and a jealous person who seems to hate her parents because she did not get enough money and assets from them. The negative reviews went on, but Helen's reaction to her upbringing shows how different people have different ways of reacting to the same challenge.

Some people blame God for their adversity, some blame others and some blame themselves, the list goes on. All this depends is on the type of counsel or input the young person growing up in challenging circumstances receives from the early stages of their lives. This can be in a strong and vibrant community that is closely knit and helps each other; they may not feel the pain of a heavy-handed parent and this may not even go on for long if others within the community picked up on the situation.

I have come to this conclusion through my personal experience of living in different communities. Closely-knit communities are likely to know what's going on in each other's home and members tend to be more open to correction and in most cases are happy to be accountable to each other. A good example of a closely-knit community is the church.

There is no better example of a closely-knit community than the church because a church environment is the ideal loving, nurturing and welcoming environment. Members tend to be caring towards one another in line with the teachings of Jesus in the bible. A good example is what is written in the bible in James chapter 2:8:

"8. If you really keep the royal law found in scripture, 'Love your neighbour as yourself, you are doing right."

A failure to love one's neighbours is a failure to do what is right in the sight of God. One would ask, what hope is there in a non-Christian and closed community with values and norms that sit well with Christian values? In Helen's book, she alludes that her culture accepts parents being heavy-handed and to treat one child better than the other. That does not, however, make the child immune to the emotional destructiveness of this form of upbringing. Helen narrates her story from a child's perspective when she describes how the emotional and physical punishment she claims to have suffered affected her life. The good news is that at least she feels she could come out of her parent's strict upbringing to live a new life in the United States of America.

Like I said before, there are many underlying reasons for the choices people make in life, and these include upbringing and one's religion. Christianity is a religion of love, forgiveness, tolerance, resilience, positivity, perseverance and hope. Not just a religion, but it is a lifestyle for believers in God who rely on the bible for guidance. I owe my very life to the various Christian individuals and groups I have mingled with throughout my stormy and early life.

By interacting with them, I learned, and I still am, to trust in God and be patient. Had they not helped me to become strong, to fight, not grow weary, not given me reasons to believe, to not give up, and helped me to carry on with my life as if everything was okay, my story would have had a totally different conclusion. I could never have done it without their relentless love and support. They taught me how to believe in God, take Him at His word and helped me to prove that the bible is truly the word of God and it works.

The BA plane my late friend Diana and I flew with landed at Heathrow on 20 September 1988. We relied on the instructions our British council advisor gave us at the Lusaka office during the briefing we had a few days before our flight. Our programme office would wait for us somewhere within the airport and so we had to find our way around Heathrow Airport to get to where he was. He was going to help us get on the train to the hotel that he had booked for us in London. We would stay there for our first week of being in United Kingdom booked to stay for one week prior to making our train journey to Reading to get to our reserved university hall accommodation. I had chosen a hall of residence closest to my university campus. I can remember the surge of excitement as we landed at the train station on our own after spending a week in the city. But before this, I remember how we couldn't find our way back to the hotel in Portobello each time we left the hotel to look around and do some shopping. Every street looked the same, but one thing I still remember is the kindness Londoners showed us. It is interesting how they could tell we were new and suspected had lost our way. It's amazing how many people talked to us and asked if we were okay and if we said no, everyone came to our rescue and directed us back to the hotel.

I remember is how in excitement; I bought this pair of shoes during one of our shopping trips and wore it the very following day unknown to me that English sizes were not quite the same as Zambian ones and besides, by September, the weather had changed and getting cooler so that shoes were not expanding as fast as they would in hot weather. My new shoes ruined my day. They hurt so much that I nearly cried and could not walk properly in them. In hindsight, I wish I removed them and just walked bare foot or even bought another pair since we were on a shopping spree. The reaction I got from the late Riana with whom I had travelled all the way from Zambia and shared the hotel room for being the best of friends and going out shopping together was harsh. She told me off nearly for wasting her time since she wanted to go to more shops. The best bit happened the very next day.

She put on her new shoes as well, having bought a pair the day I struggled with mine. As we went about around the shops, I noticed she was slowing down and losing her enthusiasm to get around as many shops as we could this being our third day of shopping in London. Her suggestion for us to return to the hotel just a few hours into our shopping day came as a surprise. Unknown to me, it was her turn to experience the pain of wearing new and tight shoes. Being the comical, witty and sneaky Diana that she was, she never disclosed her reason for wanting to go back to the hotel not long after arriving at the Portobello open market where we were to do our shopping that day.

But, when we finally got to the hotel, she burst out into this contagious, unstoppable frenzy of laughter. I have never seen her laugh so hard in my life to where she cried, and it would not surprise me is she confessed that she had also wet herself laughing. I laughed with her even before I knew why she was laughing. She could not complete a sentence without breaking out into further hysterical laughing. When she finally held a sentence together, I could not believe it when I heard her reason for wanting to come back to the hotel after just an hour or two of starting our shopping. I am sure you, by now, have guessed why our shopping spree came to a sudden end that day. It was because Diana's new shoes were tight and painful, just like mine the previous day. Good thing we knew each other well and had mutual love and respect for one another, which made the incident not a big deal.

Somehow, even in this incident, I can see how I showed a godly attitude in my reaction. I cannot claim that my reaction was pre-planned, no. But I can see God helping me to show a Christlike character to my friend, who was not saved, which is the best way of winning any unbeliever to Jesus.

Had it not been for Christ who had changed me from the old undegenerated me to the new me, who was being the Holy Spirit was continuously sanctifying, since the day I gave my life to Jesus, I was within my right to have revenged for what my friend had done to me the day before. There was no way I could have done that because revenge is not a godly reaction, and the bible teaches against it. For example, in 1 Peter 3:9, the bible says;

"9. Do not repay evil with evil or insult with

insult. On the contrary, repay evil with
blessing, because to this, you were called
so that you may inherit a blessing." (1 Peter 3:9)

This no doubt was one of the many opportunities I had to show godliness to an unsaved but very dear friend, and I will forever remain grateful to God for the opportunity to share His love with those He brought into my life and has been bringing into my life over the years and those He has continued bringing now and, in the years, to come. I would love to suggest to every Christian reader to make the most of every opportunity to share Christ's love with those who may never read the bible or enter a church building. There is a famous story that I love about a famous actor whose story of Christian faith circular television showed. His interview, which I and which to this day it is one of the best examples of Christian witnessing I have ever heard, bearing in mind this is a Hollywood star. I googled him and found an interview. Here is what this actor says, in answer to a question on how he came to faith:

He tells a story of how the family hired an au pair from somewhere in America, who the whole first week was singing in her language while working, the only language she spoke to his wife. His wife went to him and asked if he understood what she was singing about. She tells him she was singing about Jesus. She asked the au pair why every song was about Jesus. The lady had an interesting reaction. She burst out laughing and the actor's wife asked what was so funny. Then the lady said that she was not there just to clean the house but to share her faith as well and the rest is history because they both loved what she shared.

What a beautiful and inspiring story this is. If only there were a few more bold Christians not afraid to talk about their faith in their little corners, more people would come to know Jesus Christ throughout the world. We need more churches that disciple people to equip them with all that is required for effective Christian service. The good news is that not everyone can do it her way, but every Christian has an obligation to witness other Christians in their circles. The best that they can do is to use the most appropriate method of sharing the message of Jesus's love for the people of this world still lost in sin and have no hope of eternal life.

We left the hustle and bustle of London city for the town of Reading, which was much quieter than the big city back in the late eighties when I first came to England. WE arrived on Saturday and had the weekend to prepare for start of our academic year. Arriving at the Reading train station was not without its own drama. Thankfully, we got off the train all right, but we could not leave the station without help. We kept going up and down the elevator, not knowing how to get out to the bus stop. And then we found ourselves in the station's basement and kept going up the elevator, not knowing where to go. This might sound silly to you if you know about Reading or other big train stations, as you can easily work out where the exit leading to the bus stop may be.

Diana and I were not the most uncivilised women straight from some rural area of Zambia, not at all. We came from Lusaka and were familiar with escalators and fast cars, but this station still duped us. The only thing I can think of is that when excitement runs rife in someone's mind, it makes them lose the ability to stay calm and can get you thrown off by the easiest of instructions. The next saga was with the cab driver, who picked us up from the railway station to our halls of residence.

I can remember clearly getting on this black cab and remembering the false story that went around in Zambia about black cabs charging more money if you sat in a certain way. So poor Riana and I watched the clock add pound after pound and wondered whether there was anything we could do to slow the clock ticking, but we did not even try because we were tired by the time we sat down. He seemed to go around and around within the campus before finally dropping us off the student hall, which we later discovered was the nearest from the train station. Although I cannot remember how much we ended up paying, I know we paid quite a lot. Sadly, he realised how vulnerable we were and took advantage of our ignorance to make however many more pennies he milked out of us. By this time, we had spent all of our first stipend pretty much and were looking forward to the next month's instalment which served us right as it stopped us going berserk with shopping in Reading.

Windsor Castle was the first highlight for us as new students of Reading university which boasted of a large overseas student population. The university had a custom of hiring buses at the beginning of each academic year to take all new overseas students for a day's visit to the Windsor Castle. I can still recall the hype and excitement that filled the air as the buses arrived outside the student's union to pick up those new students who fancied a free bus trip to view Windsor Castle, a royal residence at Windsor in the English county of

Berkshire. On arrival there, we were at the mercy of the duty tour guides who took us from one section of the castle to another, where we saw breath-taking and beautiful ornaments of rococo, baroque and gothic value.

As someone born in Zambia, one of the copper producers of the world, something caught my attention when we entered a room decorated just in copper. I wondered how so much copper had made its way to Windsor Castle. What was its value when they brought it to England and how much is worth now, I thought to myself? Feelings of sadness hit me. I felt sad that until that day, I never appreciated something as precious as copper while I was back home. To visit Windsor as a tourist and start admiring the beauty of something that comes from the country where I was born and lived for 26 years made me feel stupid. I was born and lived in Zambia for the last 26 years of my life but thought nothing of the copper while back there. In fact, I doubt if I ever bought anything made from it. How sad?

Let me point out here that I do not have a problem with Zambia's copper being exported to England and being on display at Windsor Castle, not at all. The queen is the head of all Commonwealth countries and to be honest, if there is anyone who deserves any gifts from anyone, it is the queen. She is personally a symbol of majesty, outstanding moral standing, and godliness, never mind the chaos amongst some of her children. Of herself, the queen is a wonderful lady. She has kept her marriage to Prince Phillip, now late, as an example of good family values for the entire world. I commend her for that.

Chapter 8

My Inevitable Career Switch from Agricultural Science to Health and Social Care

Throughout this chapter, I will focus on my social care career to show the principles that influenced my elevation from care worker to care manager. First, let me tell you how I got into care before I dreamed of ever going from a hands-on carer to being a manager. As a hand-on carer, my job didn't even require me to know what the manager's office looked like, as I had no business going there. I never, ever thought a day would come when that would be my office, not in a million years. Never entering the manager's office was not because my manager operated a closed-door policy, not at all. My manager was a lovely, gentle, and genuine Christian woman. God used her and Pat Stewart, who later became my best friend, to get me hired at Helena House, a Christian provider for people with learning disabilities. To give you a better sense of the type of organization that Prospects was, let me share some things that have stuck with me about working there.

The care home we worked for, which no longer exists, was a home for Christian adults with learning difficulties started by a Baptist minister and his wife who gave birth to a child with learning difficulties. Their way of addressing the situation, difficult as it was, entailed seeking God to show them how their child would be a blessing to them and other people. The minister is an author of many books in which he shares his challenges of being a minister and those of having a child with learning difficulties.

They are the very epitome of faith through trials and my own experiences with adversity and faith through it all resonate with this minister and his wife's life experience. What attracted me to apply for a job with the company they started was because it was one of the few Christian service providers in the country. The ethos of the organisation matched the description of my dream employer. After reading the advert in a local newspaper, I did not think twice before grabbing my phone and calling to register my interest in the advertised position. It was not long after that when I started as a hands-on support worker and rose through the ranks to the post of a home manager within the same care home. That was the beginning of what I feel was the god-ordained social care career on which I had embarked. I am glad I applied for the job when I saw it and I have no regrets. Working for this Christian care provider was the best part of my social care career, although it was not without challenges like any other business or job. Unfortunately, jobs in the agricultural industry were scarce and still are for graduates in England and that has become a blessing in disguise for me, because had the agricultural jobs been readily available, I could have looked for one in line with my master's degree and missed the blessing of working and thriving as a social care professional and freelance consultant.

The main thing I want the readers to know is that even though I made the right career switch, the journey has not been easy for me as a black woman of African origin. However, the prices I have had to pay along the way have been worth their while. Despite being a graduate in another field, I had to look for jobs just to work to support my family, otherwise my family would have suffered. That was the last thing I wanted for my children. I always remembered that I had brought them to this country and it wouldn't be right to neglect them for any reason, not even the pain and sorrow of losing my family that I loved dearly. I do not think any of the people I worked and interacted with every day knew what I was going through. Whether they would have treated me any differently had they known, I cannot tell.

What matters to me is that I did what I had to do despite living with sorrow and I am grateful to God for giving me the strength to get on with life despite the loss and bereavement that I lived with. I remember the palaver that unfolded the day I was due to have my interview for the support worker's role in this company. I had forgotten about the interview and had gone to someone's hair as a side job. For those who are familiar with afro hair, you will know how creative African hairdressers can be and cleverly the make Afro hair look presentable and stylish. One of the many ways we do this is by putting the hair in single plaits with extension and intertwining the extensions together with the real hair from the scalp to the person's length of choice. This can take anything between three to 12 hours depending on many factors. In hindsight, I can see my naivety at thinking I could have done this in the six or seven hours I had before going back home to collect the kids from school.

Just as I was getting really pleased with the progress of my plaits, I got a phone call from Pat Stewart, the deputy manager of the home I would work for, who would later become a great friend, asking if I would attend the interviews at the home. Unknown to Pat, I was miles away from my home and, worse still, I had not yet started the one-hour journey from where I was to the interview venue. Had I been at my house, the journey would have taken me just under half an hour by bus under normal circumstances. Here, I relied on my customer's generosity to give me a lift once I had finished doing her hair.

On that day, I am not sure about what I was thinking. I should have known better as a competent and experienced hairdresser with years of experience working in a professional hairdressing salon owned by Janet Prior not her real name), a beautiful and laid back west Indian woman of my age with whom I became friends. I met the customer through Janet while working for her, in Reading, where her saloon was located. After getting along so well, Janet and I visited each other several times, and I even became her personal hairdresser. Not only were we of a similar age, but we had similar personalities; ambitious but not in a bad way, hardworking but not selfish, and determined in our pursuits, but still family oriented.

Janet was not married, but she had a boyfriend who I did not consider serious. Judging by the people carrier he drove, I always suspected he must have had a wife and children, but whether my friend Janet knew this, I could not tell. I remember us always sharing our concerns about him not popping the question despite being together for a long time.

My suspicions were right because the next time I met Janice, having not seen or heard from her for many years, there was a different man in her life. An Irish police officer who was clearly and madly in love with her, judging by the things she told me about him. I remember feeling so excited when she told me they spent a fair bit of time together. Knowing how she wanted to get married and start a family, I was happy for her and hoped something would come out of this relationship.

My only regret about my friendship with Janet was that I never really shared my Christian faith with her properly. But she always knew who I was and so was aware of the things I could and could not get involved in and the place I could go and those I could not go to because if I did, they would conflict with my faith. In 1 Corinthians 15 verse 33, the bible says;

"[33] Do not be misled: Bad company corrupts good character." (1 Corinthians 15:33)

Although Janice was not a Christian, she was good company to me. I have had many non-Christian friends in my life whose morals are stronger than some Christians. Am I being judgmental when I say this? Hopefully not. My goal is to share some observations I have made over the years about both born again Christians and non-Christians. The two types of friends are both human and both have feelings, but they can both choose right and wrong, and both have the freedom to make choices about how to live their lives, although those who choose to become Christians have given up this freedom, as they are called to be Christ-like and to please him rather than themselves or others.

A sense of failure grips my spirit as I relay my association with Janice in this book. I miserably failed to obey the golden command to share the word of God with others. I did not do as admonished in the bible in Romans 10:14,

"[14] How, then, can they call on the one they have not believed in? And how can they believe in the one of whom they have not heard? And how can they hear without someone preaching to them?" (Romans 10: 14)

I feel it is imperative for me to include this, and all the scriptures I have included in my book to show the readers, who perhaps are not familiar with this portion of scripture, bearing in mind, my whole book is about how knowing what the bible says about different things I have been though, that God gradually helped me to overcome these in His mercy. I want the readers to know that if God can do it for me and no doubt for many other believers, He can do it for you too. There is always the first time and the first time according to the bible is the day you hear the good news about Jesus Christ and for some this could be it; reading about my experience with adversity and how by God's grace, the adversity has not broken me, but if anything, it has built me up.

As far as my Social Care career goes, I got the job of Care Assistant in a Christian care home despite arriving for the interview at least an hour and a half late. From what I can remember, there was not much of an interview. It seemed as if all they wanted was for me to prove that I was a Christian and the rest, including gaining knowledge and skills that would come later once I had started the job. I started working as a Care Assistant at level one in July 1997 when my lastborn son was only two years and one month old.

Despite working part-time hours when I first started, I still needed reliable childcare to attend work as required and be on time. As my husband was a full time Animal Science student at Reading university, I had to juggle childcare with my part-time social care career, and this was not funny, believe me. The number of times I called to inform the shift leader that I was running late as my childcare had not arrived were countless. This was when I saw God and the hand of God upon me. I remember always leaving to go to work late on so many occasions due to childcare constraints, and this always made me feel guilty and sad. This was a defining moment for the management to draw the line between ensuring the smooth running of the home and showing me kindness. These characteristics were a test of both my manager's leadership style and her heart of compassion, but they were not in conflict with each other. This is what I meant earlier in the chapter when I said that my manager played a key role in helping me to keep my job in the Christian home where I worked. Without neglecting her professional and management responsibilities, she still showed me compassion and remained patient with me until I had sorted my childcare issues. I do not know if I could have achieved the success, I achieved in care had I not worked under a wonderful, caring and understanding manager who supported me in every way they could when I struggled with childcare. I may never have continued working at Helena House and may never have risen to the position of manager that I rose to while there. It was the love and care and relentless support I received from management and other staff that inspired me to give my job the best shot, not knowing I was setting myself up for something I have imagined was possible when I took up the Care Assistants job back in July 1997.

After working as a day carer for a couple of years, the Local Authority approved night care funding, and I was the first employee that they offered night work, as it would work well with taking care of my baby during the day. A deep sense of relief came over me when I heard they had confirmed me as a night carer. As expected, it worked well since the night shifts were not too busy initially apart from the occasional moments when one or two woke up and wondered, but nothing too much. If I said I never closed my eyes during my night care worker assignment at this care home, I would be lying. I know I used to sit on a comfortable green sofa to read a book when it was quiet and without a doubt, I may have fallen asleep, although not a deep sleep, like being in one's bed at home. My two years of working as a night carer at Helena House were the best two years I spent there. I made so many friends with whom I used to pray the night away. I remember praying with Pet Stew, Claire Andrews, Jo Ray, and with my late friend Janine Lowe. My prayer ties with Janine were special. I can remember us praying for members of our families and some of the staff for God to do whatever needed to be done for them. I remember praying for a male carer who stayed single until his late thirties when we realised, he wanted to get married until we got wind of his engagement to a Christian woman he had suddenly met somewhere. This brought Janine and I immeasurable joy and encouraged us to continue interceding for anyone we heard had a challenge. We prayed for a young woman who had a problem that arose in her marriage until we heard things had improved. We prayed most of the night, which meant that Janine would report for work the next day having slept little and I know this sounds irresponsible, but somehow, she went through the day and returned to work the next day.

Chapter 9

God Moves in the Most Unprecedented Way and Opens a Door of Promotion

Regarding my promotion, it came in the most unusual way. The manager who employed me moved on and a new manager succeeded her, who also moved on to start a family, before a third manager who succeeded her also moved on. So, I worked under three different manager's is the space of six years of working for Prospects. In hindsight, I can see my social care career path in the light of a bible verse that talks about God knowing the thoughts He has for us; good thoughts to us, a hope and a future. This right here describes God's promises to me personally, and I have proved that believing what He says and personalising it even before you see the manifestation is a good habit to develop. On the reverse, I cannot claim that I could see the sweet smell of success before my promotion because I could not. All thanks to Roger Darch, a Devonshire man who became my third manager, a wonderful man like none I had seen the likes of in an Englishman outside my church circles. I worked as his deputy and I prayed for him on one occasion when he became ill and God healed him, to all our surprise, just like that. The story about me arriving at work one day just to be told I needed to drive to his house to take the handover to take up the position of acting manager due to him being critically ill is another story for another day. He handed over to me. I asked if I could pray for him before leaving his house, to which he said yes, and the rest is history. I started acting as manager with no preparation of any sort and thought I would act only until he came back, something we all thought would not happen as his medical report was not good. It said he did not have long to live; in which case they would look for a suitable replacement. When Roger became my manager, he continued showing me the same level of kindness that his predecessors, especially my first manager Pam, had shown me. He helped to help me keep my job when I had childcare issues. As the deputy manager in the year, I started working for the same organisation with him, he would be in the building mostly when I called to apologise for running late. He would appeal to the others on shift to bear with me and do what they could until I arrived to take my position wherever they had assigned me to work that day, on the ground floor with four occupants or on the first floor with six occupants.

It was Roger who interviewed me for climbing up the first level of the career ladder at Helena House when I applied to become a Care Assistant Level 2 and later Care Assistant Level 3, as I had no interview for my manager position. I remember him interviewing with a senior level manager from Head Office, also a gentle, caring, and respectable gentleman. They both felt that it would not be a great idea for me to jump from being a night care assistant to level three and held back from offering me that post and offered me the level two instead. They advised me to apply for the level three in a few months if I felt ready to do so, I could have another go, which I did and succeeded the second time around. I later took over from Roger when he resigned and joined another company, although he came back after a few years of being away and became the manager of another service that belonging to the same company.

This is precisely I became the manager of Helena House in 2003. The surprising thing is that I had no formal qualifications for the role. It had to be God's favour and His plans for me for such a fascinating career path to happen. The God of wonders did it for me against all odds.

England, a Levelling Place for All

I have heard the pastor of my church makes this statement; 'Heaven is a levelling place for everyone on a number of occasions. He is 101 percent right. When we get to heaven, there will be huge surprises for many people. It will not be the rich in the eyes of this world that will find mansions waiting for them to occupy, but those who have invested in their heavenly future who will find mansions waiting for their occupancy for eternity. To start delving into how to invest in our future in heaven will be a slight diversion from the real purpose of this chapter as it will require quite research to make sure I fully understand all those things that one needs to do to invest in heaven.

My pastor's statement reflects a similar truth relating to the observation I made about foreigners living in England. As a foreigner, England was a levelling place in the '80s and '90s. Degrees were not worth much in England back then. Even graduates used to make a living doing menial jobs like cleaning, care, customer service in supermarkets, as warehouse operatives. and for the few who would have been in the nation long, nursing. The highly educated foreigners, especially from Africa, including those with PhDs, Masters and bachelor's degrees or other qualifications, fall in the same category as the untrained. All did the jobs mentioned earlier in this paragraph. In contrast with Africa and other developing countries where the educated people love people to be acknowledge their big titles and love to show off their academic achievements, most African PhD holders did not identify themselves for fear of looking incompetent. In those days, earning enough money to pay bills and put food on the table for their families was all that mattered. There was a period in my early days in England when I could not even afford to take my children to the playground which was less than five minutes' walk from my house because I was too tired.

This may be a revelation to you, readers, to hear that immigrant, work from hand to mouth in the first few years of trying to settle in a foreign country, like England. Their focus to start with is normally to pay household bills and have enough to live on. Not so with those who were born and bred in England. The majority include a holiday somewhere in the sun on the list of their key priorities. Few Africans can afford or even think of going on holiday. Sad to say, most work round the clock and all year round without taking a break and they do not appear to get phased by this. All they wish for is to earn sufficient income to put food on the table and have a roof over their head and stay debt free. Travelling home to see their families, if they can afford the air ticket, is their holiday.

Unfortunately, this status quo affects most African immigrants to Europe regardless of their level of education.

Turns and Twists of Life in England: An Encounter with Bailiffs

I want to provide background information on bailiffs for readers who may not know what they do. These men are enforcement agents who collect a debt for goods or money owed to organisations they represent. They are vicious, forceful, and scary. They are usually big men who put on a serious appearance, and they use a curt and laconic communication style to put pressure on and get whoever finds themselves at their mercy. No one wants to cross their path if they can help it. They can cause anyone to have a brain freeze and get clammy. It is a scary thing to hear the word terms, "law enforcement officers or bailiff" on opening the door in answer to the doorbell on realising that they deliver a fatal blow. You do not want them at your door, believe me. They are bearers of unwelcome news and they put up a front that says, 'I don't care, and yet underneath, most do.'

I had an encounter with one recently when one of my sons fell behind in his university accommodation rent when he lived in an expensive area of London. That was when I realised even bailiffs are sot people at heart. They may come across as vicious and tough, but in fact, underneath, they have feelings of compassion, especially if they believe you are telling the truth. When they came to my door one day, I was upstairs getting ready for work. They have a habit of catching people before they leave their houses at dawn. In my case, I was in process of getting ready for work, aiming to leave the house by 7:30 a.m. at the latest, when one of my sons called out to me from downstairs.

I still remember the mixed feeling that run through my mind as I realised what we were in for. This bailiff made a mistake when he ordered my son, who lived at home, to get their brother, who was at university doing his last year in IT on the phone. That was when the protective instinct of a mother suddenly welled up in me. I felt controlled anger, which I know we are all capable of exercising, take over my usual quiet self. I excused myself and grabbed the mobile phone off my son, who was trying to tell his university brother something to do with bailiffs. My son was at the time in the middle of preparing for exams. I told my son not to worry and promised to call him later and faced the Bailiff, remembering who I was in Christ and knowing my son may have been in the wrong.

I then turned to the bailiff and politely requested him never to send any letters or make any calls to my son while he was at university, as that would distress him and affect his studies. Then I said that I did not feel that it would be of benefit to anyone. By this time, I had come to my senses and realised what had just transpired. What I had said to my son over the telephone moved the bailiff. To cut the long story short, the bailiff apologised to my university son and told him he would do everything he could within his power to stop anyone ever calling him again, especially now that he knew he was studying and had exams and, since I, his mother had pledged to assist him clear the debt. He then said these truly kind words to me; 'Sophie, I am sorry for disturbing your son. I promise, I will never again ask to speak to him or send any letters to him while he is at university. I will deal with you

112

directly until your son leaves university.' Then he asked me what I could afford to pay that day and we made a deal which I kept and cleared a £5000 debt within three months.

There are two important points I want to make in connection with my son's debt and the encounter we had with the bailiff on that fateful day. The first point relates to getting into debt. How did my son incur such an enormous debt in just one year of being at university and yet I used to support him, on top of a small student grant he had at the beginning of the year? From my understanding, my son got into the same habits fresher's fall into when they manage what appears to them as enormous amounts of money for the first time when they receive their stipend. To a young person, having to manage money for the first time can appear straightforward and easy, but it is not. When your student loan arrives, it feels like manna from heaven.

Unless a student has had guidance from family or by accessing and reading the wealth of information in libraries and online, they are bound to make the same mistake that many have made repeatedly. It is often not until that sweet stash of cash has disappeared, and it disappears swiftly, that it dawns on too many a student what they have done. This is because most of them did think about money or budgeting before, especially if they lived at home with their parents and may not have had a job before coming to university. My son was no exception. I found that he had gone wild with shopping for new shoes, Nintendo games and take away before setting aside rent money. It is no wonder the bible says:

"6 Train up a child in the way he should go,
[a] and when he is old he will not depart from it."
(Proverbs 22:6)

Had his father and I, or even his older siblings taken the trouble to sit him down and talk to him about expenditure and how not to get into debt when he got to university, he may not have got into the money troubles he got into. The question to ask is, how many parents, regardless of our status and/or nationality, take the trouble to give their children guidance on how to conduct themselves when they go to university for the first time? Not many do which means that the number of those who do not surpass the number of those who do. To an extent, I blame myself for the bailiff situation that befell my family, as I have already pointed out. We brought it on ourselves by not taking steps to mentor our son for his benefit and for ours as well.

Working from Hand to Mouth

The second point I want to make will back my first point about African families working day and night and living from hand to mouth. There are two implications of life. First, it means that most immigrant parents hardly ever spend time with our children and therefore do not really teach them valid lessons of life that our parents taught us when we were growing up. Aside from instructing our children, we have no time to monitor them so that if they appear to be going off the hook, we can support them fittingly and make timely corrections just as the bible verse in Proverbs 22: 6 above says. Second, since in most cases we work from hand to mouth, sad to say, it is impossible to save for the rainy day. Had I not been through paying mountains and mountains of debt for many other family members, I would have had enough to clear my son's rent just on the day the bailiff called, but the truth of the matter is I wasn't and besides, I had bought a ticket to visit my son and his wife abroad and have some sort of holiday, something that I enjoy doing even though holiday making is not a typical feature within the African culture.

Chapter 10

Buying Our First Home

When I came to England, I came to study at university. I did not really have any plans on how we, as family were going to establish ourselves in England, considering this was a freight country. Buying a house was the remotest of thoughts I had in my mind. It, in fact, surprised me when I first came across an African who had bought his own house in England. I could not work out how possible this was. In Zambia, my mother forced me to buy a house because she did not believe in renting. As far as she could see, every college graduate had the potential to buy their own house, so she kept pushing my sisters and me to buy our own houses until I did just to please her. If there are any regret I have, it is for not getting on the Zambian property ladder much sooner. My mother had found me a house through a builder she knew who wanted to sell quickly as he was unwell and, sadly, he died.

I lost this house even though I had paid a part of the money towards buying it because someone connived with the builder and gave them a bit of money as well and got the title deeds for it. My mum tried to fight for the house, but to no avail. I cannot understand my thinking then. Mum wrote to warn me about someone who wanted to steal the house she had already secured on my behalf. I did nothing about it. The only thing I remember attempting to do was to solicit the help of Mum's cousin, who was an MP of his province, to see if he could use his influence to get the house back for us. This did not work, as I lived a day's journey away in another province.

Coming to think of it, it is possible the man that took the house had not even paid a penny but since the vendor had passed away, there was no way of proving anything. That house is gone now, and I am not the one to cry over spilt milk. I believe in letting things go and starting afresh. This incident reminds me of the story of Isaac and Gerer's servants fighting over the wells that Gerer's servants claimed from Isaac's servants. I love the conclusion of the story.

"[19] Isaac's servants dug in the valley and discovered a well of fresh water there. [20] But the herders of Gerer quarrelled with those of Isaac and said, 'The water is ours!' So, he named the well, Esek,[c] because they disputed with him. [21] Then they dug another well, but they quarrelled over that one also; so he named it Sitnah.[d] [22] He moved on from there and dug another well, and no one quarrelled over it. He named it Rehoboth,[e] saying, 'Now the Lord has given us room and we will flourish in the land.'" (Genesis 27:19–22 NIV)

That's what makes the bible unique and sets its followers apart. There are stories in it about the people of old who, for the fear of God, wanted to live in peace and would go to any length to do so, just as shown in the story of Isaac and Gerer above. It teaches people to be forgiving and never to get revenge. It paints a picture that might appear like Christians have a 'loser mentality' and yet, Christians know they lose to win. Just as Isaac said in the last statement in the scripture above, God is bound to reward all those who refrain from revenge and self-vindication at last, and I have seen this in my own life. An example that comes to mind is that of a time when I became a member of a subcommittee of one charity that I was a member of. The chairperson ordered me to step down for missing a meeting by the then chair of that committee, and so I did. Before long, members elected me to be the chair of the main committee that oversaw the sub-committee that had dismissed me for not attending one or two meetings. Why am I telling this story in my book? I am including this story to show how careless, spiritually insensitive Christians can sometimes be hurtful towards others, especially those who are going through challenging times. Had the chairperson of the committee alluded to in this incident bothered to find out my reason for not attending the one or two meetings that I missed, she may not have taken the decisions she took to dismiss me. In the meantime, I was hurting even though I chose not to isolate myself from social activities but continued taking part in whatever activities I felt would benefit me and others.

When I became the chairperson of the main charity committee, one member of the sub-committee surprised me. She spoke kindly and encouraged me with these words; 'Sophie, watch this space. God is going to bless you beyond your wildest dream because you have accepted to accept this appointment. You will even buy a house for your family.' To be honest, her positivity, as it sounded then, was just a pie in the sky because our household income was exceptionally low, and we had no savings. Buying a house was out of reach for us as we would never have raised the deposit, even if we were to save for the next few years.

I might have forgotten all that this kind Christian sister said to me, but after a while, I am not sure what came over me after hearing someone indirectly say; some people pray a lot, but they have nothing to show for their faith. That hit me line a tonne of bricks and I said to myself, I need to stop people mocking me because of my faith in God. The statement upset me as it sounded to me, they were insulting my God.

I was determined to prove the person wrong, so while the provocation was rife, I started praying to God to help me raise the finance to buy our own house. I particularly remember attending another meeting where someone else made another unkind and mocking statement about Christian with nothing to show for their faith. This is what they said: 'Some people pray a lot and seem to be anointed, but how come they have nothing to show for it?' How come God is not blessing them materially? Anointing without money is anointing.'

That set me off. I thought to myself, this an insult to my heavenly father, and am I going to seek His face and pray, asking Him to glorify Himself in my life and change any areas of my life that bring shame on His Holy name! I did exactly what Hannah did when she was upset by Peninnah because Hannah was barren until the tide turned for her after prayer. They were both wives of the same husband. Peninnah kept conceiving and giving birth, while nothing happened to Hannah. When she perceived Hannah was barren, Peninnah started mocking her. In 1 Samuel 1: 6–16 it goes like this:

"6. Peninnah teased Hannah to make her angry. She did it because the LORD had kept Hannah from having children." (Samuel 1:6 NKJV)

This is one of the most amazing bible stories on God's faithfulness to answer the prayers of anyone that prays fervently. It is such a privilege to make it a part of my book and my wish to leave it as it is for the reader to enjoy this story. I prayed specifically for material blessings, especially for a house. I went into a praying spree if there is anything like that and I was determined to pray until the Lord answered my prayer. Then I started hunting for a house to buy even though I had no deposit. I drove around viewing one house after another for over a year. The funny thing is that while searching for the right house, I had a knowing in my heart that my time to buy a house had come, even though I did not know how I would raise the deposit.

I remember my friend, Carla Alves telling me about a housing scheme, and she even gave me the telephone number to call to help me find and try out many other housing schemes. Eventually, in 2007, I found a house to buy from a Housing Association that needed little money to set the process going. By this time, I was earning enough that made our combined enough to qualify for a mortgage.

In the meantime, my church was praying with us, and I started asking people to pray for us each time I attended prayer meetings. After praying for months, I had a dream. I dreamt that my best friend, Joy Reid, and I were at an auction taking place in open ground. I remember us sitting on green grass in front of a sizeable group of people bidding for a house. Suddenly, I saw two pieces of white paper wrapped around the handle of the property that was on auction. I crept forward to read the words written on them. To my surprise, one of them had my first name written on it; and the second one had my surname. I came back and told Joy, who signalled to me to keep quiet and not say anything to stop other bidders hearing what I was telling her.

I remember a white woman in her thirties sitting in front of Jo and I in the dream as if she were first on the queue. When I woke up, I thought little about the dream until after we bought the house. I found out from the vendor's father who was showing me around when I came to view the house with my friend Jan Bismuth that someone else had already taken the house. Something strange happened that day. As I walked in through the front door, a sense of peace came over me and I knew God was trying to confirm something to me.

The housing association wrote to me to tell me they had not offered me the house as someone else had taken it. I travelled to South Africa to represent my charity on a mission field organised by a church in Hampshire where the director of the charity used to be a member. After being away for days, I received an emergency call from my husband informing me that the housing association had sent a letter to the house asking me to get in touch within a set period to confirm if I still wanted the house.

What? This cannot be true because as far as I was concerned, they had sold the house sold to someone else. But, when God says yes, as the songwriter puts it, nobody can say no for sure. Prior to all this, I remember stepping forward for prayer at the end of a sermon delivered by Doctor Isaiah, who was a guest speaker in my church for the day. The year he visited us, Dr Isiah was the principle of the Nairobi Bible College, which has connections with my church. He specifically prayed that God would surprise me and give my family the best. Months passed after that, a sister from church had a dream that my family had moved into a beautiful house on a farm. As the Lord would have it, we bought a detached house built in 2003, in September 2007.

Who says that God does not answer prayers? Of course, He does, especially desperate prayers of His people who have no one else to grant them their requests. Today, I live in a house that God Himself provided the means for us to get. Although I was still heart broken and still hurting, I never gave up on God, never stopped praying and have had so many prayers answered. The whole idea for authoring this book is to share with the reader how our pains draw us closer to God and remind everyone that even after losing dear ones, we should remember that life goes on. You still need to work to pay rent or buy a house. We still need to read the bible, go to church, and do other normal things; if we allowed the spirit of grief to overtake us, we could achieve nothing, may never recover from it and we would end up being worthless in the eyes of the world. I doubt that our loved ones who have passed on would want us to amount to nothing. I believe they would want to see us succeed and have the best life, even in their absence. Thanks be to God that with His help, I am not just existing in life, but living a fulfilled and decent life, despite missing my ten siblings and parents. If I live, I am determined to be effective in the lives of others going through one form of adversity or the other. For me, it is not just about material wealth, but also about spiritual, physical and emotional well-being for everyone around me. I will always pray for strength and ask God to make me a blessing, not only to my immediate family but to all the people, as He will bring my way.

When praying for a house to buy, I remembered a message preached by a dear female minister, now deceased, sometime back on praying for the right place to move to when moving about to a new house. That stayed with me. In her preaching, she warned that the chances that you end up in a rough neighbourhood are high if you do not pray to God for direction. I can testify to the glory of God that I live in a quiet area where most people are business owners, with hardly any youngsters shouting and fighting along the road. There is no loud music and no speeding cars, just the normal traffic of both vehicles and people. I am so grateful to God for leading me to my current place of residence.

I put that down to God for answering that prayer. I have heard of neighbours from hell, and I can truthfully say, apart on one odd occasion when I found what I thought was rubbish from a bathroom bin; it contained a toilet tissue packaging, baby wipes and toothpaste cartons on the side of my fence one day when tidying up the garden.

That upset me, but as a Christian, we pattern our lives after the bible; remembering the bible verse in James that talks about not allowing ourselves to be angry for too long, I had to pray for peace and had to forgive the neighbour if they had done it as I couldn't say for sure that they had done it deliberately. The bible says;

"25. Therefore, each of you must put off falsehood and speak truthfully to his neighbour, for we are members of one another. 26. Be angry, yet do not sin. Do not let the sun set upon your anger. 27. And do not give the devil a foothold."

(Ephesians 4:26)

"25. Therefore, each of you must put off falsehood and speak truthfully to his neighbour, for we are members of one another. 26. Be angry, yet do not sin. Do not let the sun set upon your anger. 27. And do not give the devil a foothold." (Ephesians 4:26)

Remember, I connected this incident to an unpleasant incident that I had with a neighbour, making this bible verse is simply perfect for meditation. I thank God that I may have reacted to the situation, but I did what I could within my strength not to behave unbecomingly and make my neighbour speak against God and church goers. I know too well how quick people are to blame God for the conduct of Christians that does not portray Christian values. It is as if when one becomes a Christian, they become saints overnight, which is fallacy. I thank God that I have a good relationship with this same neighbour and even asked my church to pray for her sister and mother when they were ill. I always make sure I say hello to each time I see them. There's peace on our street and this is great because I pray for everyone living along it.

Chapter 11

Challenges at Work as a Black Manager

I wish I could say my social care career has been a heaven on earth experience and that it has been plain sailing, but I would lay if I did. I can, however, say that I thank God for making a way for me because if He did not, there was no way I could have achieved the success that I had have achieved in Social Care if God was not behind my success.

I have a principle that I apply to my vocational commitments and my service to God by serving others. It is a bible principle. We found this verse in the book of Colossians 3:23–24, which says: "23;

"Whatever you do, work at it with your whole being, for the Lord and not; 24. because you know that you will receive an inheritance from the Lord as your reward. It is the Lord Christ you are serving." (Colossians 3:23–24 NIV)

That scripture speaks volumes and makes me think about tasks in a sombre manner. When I accept to do a task, be it at work, church, or to a certain extent, at home for my family, I do it whole heartedly, and if I cannot, I will say so. I always say to myself, if the bible says it, then I have no choice but to do it not out of fear but out of reverence for God and absolute conviction that His word is infallible, and it has a power to cause things to happen or prevent things from happening. I am not for one second claiming that I have arrived, not at all. All I am trying to say is that I am striving to become a better person and a loyal follower of Jesus Christ by doing everything I can within my strength to live by bible principles.

One challenge I faced when I embarked on a professional development journey was the opposition I faced from other staff. There was something that made people treat me with contempt and disregard my authority. I had to deal with so much insubordination that when I look back, I cannot understand how I did it, but I know without a doubt that God helped me. I can remember the first time they made me a shift leader to run the late shift at the Christian care home I worked, which used to be a home for adults with learning difficulties. The staff on duty would display a 'go slow' type performance on me in protest of my appointment to shift leading duties.

The home's layout is such that it spread over two floors and so, we would split the team into two, one for each floor, and it was the responsibility of each team to complete all the tasks on their floor. However, sadly for me, those placed on the ground floor did not complete all the duties, knowing it would be the responsibility of the shift workers to clear unfinished duties before leaving at the end of a shift that ran from 2 to 10 p.m. Bearing in mind, I was a very tender and touchy person as I was still dealing with the loss of my siblings and my dad, but nobody knew this. I hid it well because I was not the one to mourn and openly seek attention from others. I had developed copying mechanisms which included working non-stop so I could forget my sorrows.

I sang as I worked, read magazines, did word puzzles, watched quizzes, went out for walks, made telephone calls, and went out with friends. Whatever was applicable depended on where I was, who I was with, what was going on, the time of day and the day of the week. I must admit, all these things helped to drown my sorrow and keeping me focused, but for a moment inside, I was still hurting, but I never gave up hope. One of the best things I did was to attend church meetings and listen to preachers and join in singing songs of praise to God.

As God would have it, church stuff was part of the work schedule at this care home; being a Christian home, I thrived in it. I enjoyed my job and did so well that my performance pleased my managers. That led to my promotion from Support Worker Level One, working my way up the ranks to Support Worker Level Two, and then Three, and lastly as a deputy manager before becoming the manager in less than two years of my elevation.

Being a Home Manager entailed travelling a minimum of four times a year and staying for two nights each time attending three-day seminars. It meant that I had to travel to other parts of the country where managers from other parts of the country had not really worked with or even come across a black manager. Now, remember that I am sensitive because of the grief I am undergoing and the people I am interacting with do not know it. That meant that I had to put up a front without realising it to appear normal.

Little did I realise I appeared tense and timid and often found it difficult to join in conversations and where people deliberately or unconsciously made what I interpreted as racist remarks. It hurt inside, but I did not react. I must, however, have got tensed up, appeared bleak, and chagrined, I do not know. But I could tell from the way the people looked at me it was not only me that sensed the tense air and noticed the careless words, whether spoken unintentionally or intentionally, to make a point that I was in the wrong place.

I remember attending a senior management workshop in 2009 at the Hayes Conference Centre when one of the new managers stood up on the last day of the workshop and made this statement; 'Has anyone seen a black bag lying about in a wrong place anywhere?' As she made this statement, she stood near me and looked in my direction. All I can remember is the dead silence that followed and praying in my heart for strength. The disappointing thing about such people and their racist or just careless behaviour is that nobody ever does anything about it and often, even the victims of their racist slurs never really take it anywhere and the reason is that few employers have stringent measures in place to deal with such things.

I know I did nothing to address that kind of treatment when I experienced it simply because I did not feel supported back then. Remember, I was hurting at the time and things like that used to add salt to my wounds. However, as a Christian, my negative experience never shook my faith in God. God always got me thorough difficult moments like these. Prayer became my lifestyle and I know that there were many a time when somehow, as soon as there was a display of racism against me or somebody else, each time incidents like happened, God would move on people around me from the same social circles to cancel them out by speaking exceedingly kind words to me. I remember during the same seminar working up and dreading the thought of going to the dining hall for breakfast. But somehow, I plucked courage from somewhere inside me, left my room and went towards the dining hall. Then, as I was heading towards the dining hall, a director walked straight to me and asked if they could give me a hug in full view of other delegates. That was definitely God stepping in to show me He was watching over me, showing me, He loved me, and He can use His obedient servants to show His love to those in need of reassurance, as He did for me that day.

After moving on from the Christian organisation, I joined a London based provider for the same client group. Despite being non-Christian provider, I did not face near enough as racism and rejection as I did when I worked for a Christian company. It is important for me to mention that there were committed Christians who were welcoming to me and other employees from the ethnic minority group. These people did their best to show me and others in my position love and acceptance despite our racial differences. It would not be right for me to paint everyone with the same brush just because of the minority who, although claimed to be Christians themselves, were racist. Their racist attitude made it difficult for them to accept people of different ethnicities.

Had I not been a mature Christian when all these were going on in my life, I could have struggled to accept that even believers in Jesus Christ can fall short of Christian standards because they are human, prone to temptations and can show ungodly behaviours and succumb to temptations. The beauty of all this is that despite facing racism from an insignificant number of colleagues, there were more who displayed true Christian values because of their love for Jesus, and their unquestionable allegiance to Him and His ways. These are the people that genuinely love the Lord and do all they can to apply bible principles to how they live their daily lives just as the bible puts it in 1 John 3:3–4

"We know that we have come to know him if we keep his commands. 4. Whoever says, 'I know him,' but does not do what he commands is a liar, and the truth is not in that person." (1John 3:3-4)

These bible verses define Christian living. I always refer to them each time I feel concerned about my relationship with other Christians. I always ask God to forgive me if I feel I have failed to love others as the bible puts it in these verses. It gives me a cause for concern when I see Christians claiming to love God, but in the meantime, they blatantly declare their dislike for other people, regardless of their reason for it.

While visiting my son Danny and his dear wife, doctor Paulina in New Zealand, my daughter-in-law asked me a question about interacting with gay people. She wanted to gauge my attitude towards them, knowing who I was. I cannot remember the exact answer I gave her, but I must have tried to avoid the subject at all costs for fear of falling short of political correctness and sounding judgemental. I may have even said I hated all sexual sin because of the devastation it causes families, although I love the people just as recorded in Jude 1:23:

"Rescue others by snatching them from the flames of judgment. Show mercy to still others, but do so with great caution, hating the sins that contaminate their lives."
(Jude 1:23 NLT)

What she told me after listening to me really humbled me. She told me of what she had heard from a minister somewhere about loving gay people like any other sinner and cautiously sharing the word of God with them without condemning them; if we care otherwise, they will not see the error of their ways and so may end off in hell, if what the bible says about homosexuality is anything to go by and as we all know, it sure is. If anyone wants to know what God says about sexuality, in the bible in the book of Romans 1:26, for anyone interested in finding out. The main thing is not to judge, as the bible says in James 4:12; "12.

"There is only one Lawgiver and Judge, the one who is able to save and destroy. But you – who are you to judge your neighbour?" (James 4:12 NASB)

Why am I relating homosexuality to a failure to show a lack of Christian love? I am trying to show that sometimes Christians display ungodly and therefore unacceptable attitudes towards other people. This should not be the case. We should always remember that everyone is the same in the eyes of God, male and female, black and white, rich, and poor, and sin is sin, whether it be sexual sin which includes homosexuality, adultery, fornication, stealing, lying, murder, idolatry, and all the sins listed in the Galatians chapter from 5:22 onwards. Justifying any behaviours that violate the law of God and neither is not right. It is a failure to obey God's instructions that exhort us to love one another, just like Jesus taught. We obviously cannot do it on our own, but God has promised to give us power to overcome all sins through the help of His word and the work of the Holy Spirit. In Galatians 5: 16–18, here is what the bible says;

"16. So I say, walk by the Spirit, and you will not gratify the desires of the flesh. 17. For the flesh desires what is contrary to the Spirit, and the Spirit what is contrary to the flesh. They are in conflict with each other, so that you are not to do whatever[c] you want. 18. But if you are led by the Spirit, you are not under the law. The acts of the flesh are listed in." (Galatians 5:16–25 NIV)

It makes an interesting reading for those who wish to check it out. We can see from the two portions of scripture quoted one after the other that it takes the help of the Holy spirit for us to overcome the desires of the flesh that are listed in Galatians 5:19–22 and as written in the succeeding verses 23–24, accepting Jesus into our hearts and making Him not only our saviour but our Lord as well, so we become his followers and live by His word and forsake our own ways for His sake so that He will accept us in His heaven when we die.

For me, as I sought healing from the pain of the loss of my siblings and my father, I learned to depend upon God more and more and in doing so, reading the bible and finding facts of life that I may not have found in a million years had I not made a personal decision to live a Christian life by trying my best to find out more about the God of the bible and try to apply bible principles to everything I did.

I am deliberately using multiple bible verses because I want the readers to read the references I have made in context. I want to make it easy for anyone who may not be familiar with the layout of the bible to read the scripture I have used without the need to google them or open a bible. It is imperative that I quote scriptures otherwise, it will be impossible for me to tell the story of the journey of loss, bereavement, and healing that I have been on, considering the bible has been my main source of comfort and point of reference when I needed guidance and something to hold on to. Try it for yourself and you will not regret it.

I remember joining a franchise as the Registered Care Manager for a branch local to me. I will never forget the shock that hit me one day when the owner made a racist statement right in my face while discussing the documents of another foreigner's identification documents. We had recruited new caregivers and were verifying their documents before offering them job contracts. The director got frustrated that the Disclosure and Barring Services (DBS) certificate for new employees born and bred in the United Kingdom did not receive the privileged treatment they deserve, but a foreign national certificate came out in no time.

This annoyed the director. He then made the statement that shocked me. He said, 'Why should this person's certificate get issued so quickly and yet those of English applicants are not yet ready?' This confused me because I expected him to be pleased that at least one new employee was ready to work instead of complaining about it. When I asked his reason for getting annoyed about the fact that a foreign worker had received their paperwork, he blatantly said because she is a foreigner. I thought, What? At that point, I realised that as a foreigner myself, I may have been an annoyance and not an asset to him. I knew from that day that the only reason he had employed me was because he had got to a point of no return when trying to get a manager because the first manager, he had offered the job to have declined the offer and so he had no choice but to accept to see me when an agency forwarded my CV to him. There was nothing he could do about the level of experience I had by the time he met me and as he was running out of time, he needed a manager to recruit a manager to meet a head office deadline for a new business owner and manager induction.

The incident I just shared changed my entire outlook on him and made me overly cautious. It is no wonder, when later in the year, we recruited a care coordinator who became blatantly disrespectful and portrayed insubordination towards me; he did nothing to support me and to stop it. I remember the day that sealed my fate that a new employee in her fifties, walked in the shared open plan office space we used to share and ignoring me, yet she had come to see in the first place, she walked to the coordinator and blatantly made a racist statement before the two of them burst out laughing. The director heard them, pretended he never heard them, and continued as if nothing had happened.

It hurt, but I put on a brave face and waited for their racist banter to end before I asked her to pass the documents, she had brought for processing to me. She passed the documents to me but never said a word; no hello or sorry or anything like that. She then continued talking to the coordinator and involved the director in the conversation, but totally disregarded me. The good news is that by this time, I had summoned God-given courage and not only put on a brave face but took charge and spoke out.

I cannot remember what I said but I know it was in the line of reminding her who she should deal with the next time she came to the office and I may have also added that she should please remember the coordinator might be her friend, but I was the manager and so I handled certain aspects of running the business. Silence at last. The coordinator peered through the small space between the visitor and the filing cabinets to look at me, saying nothing.

This kind of behaviour went on and on until it became the order of the day. The coordinator would discredit me in front of junior staff by talking over me when dealing with different issues with staff who had come to the office and even trying to take calls when people called to speak to the manager until I felt if I did nothing, that sort of behaviour would continue. I stopped her the next time she tried to take my call and told her to stop doing my job because she was unqualified. She nearly put my name and the organisation in disrepute when she failed to pass a matter that she did not know how to address just because she had made the person involved believe she was in charge and so tried addressing the issue without asking for advice from me. That was the day I decided I needed to stop the behaviour and so when a call came in, I listened to the conversation ready to take over in the call related to my job role saying to myself, if it is anything relating to my job role, I will ask her to hand over the phone.

And sure enough, a call came and as before, she tried to respond to a matter that was not her responsibility to respond to; at that point, I stood up from my desk and firmly but politely asked her to pass the telephone to me, and reminded her to always pass all calls connected to management decisions and responding to management queries to me.

I wish I could say that she learned her lesson, but no, she never. Things got from bad to worse, but the director did nothing about it. The word black and foreigner made the main vocabulary of the day in our office, over the phone, face to face with the few caregivers she had connived with until I felt concerned that the possibility of deliberately doing things to implicate me was imminent.

The director disposition changed from that of a professional and supportive man that I met when I joined the organisation to someone who openly challenged my leadership during team meetings and made statements like, 'This is my business and so I can do what I like.' I knew it was time to move on and so I gave my notice exactly after two years of working for the company.

Here is my point; the owner of the care agency I ran was without a doubt a nice man. But one may ask; how come he made statements like those he made? The answer is simple; there were many nice people who do not know how to feel about the growing numbers of outsiders coming into their nations regardless of where this may be, and different people react to different triggers at different times. To think that there will ever be a time when racism and other group identity problems are over is like a dream that may never come.

I have learned how to deal with situations like these better as I grew older and I have found out that it is better to defuse certain situations, even if we feel unjustly treated. Taking certain measures and applying wisdom when responding to these things in the way of doing things, bearing in mind that two wrongs do not make a right. Looking at this from a Christian point of view, I can say that praying about things but also acting is important to prevent all kinds of abuse. Not reporting abuse to authorities so they could act on the incidents cost me dearly in the past.

I am not suggesting for a minute that when we report cases of abuse to authorities, they will deal with them successfully, not at all. However, when report these things, we pass the onus to act on them to the leadership. Also, as a Christian, I missed the excellent opportunity to put bible teachings into practice. The bible teaches that we should do everything within our strength to live in peace with one another. My pastor always says, 'Love wins.' Romans 12:18 says;

> "[18] If it is possible, as far as it depends
> on you, live at peace with everyone."
> Romans 12:18(NIV)

I may have been reacting the way I did over the years because of the pain that I live with that had made sensitive. It may have been all part of the grieving process I had been dealing with all along, expressing itself through elevated levels of sensitivity I showed now and again. I do not know for sure, but even if it were, I still needed to do something about it, otherwise it could have ruined my career. Here is my point.

Undergoing loss and bereavement does not excuse us from conducting ourselves appropriately in our work situations and neither does it protect us from further hurts. It makes us sensitive and vulnerable. This opens us up for further abuse and rejection by those who could not care less whether we were happy and bubbly or sad. It is down to us to be strong and refuse to be punch bags for unkind and angry people. We need to take action to protect ourselves from further hurts.

Remember that the world is not a perfect place. It is a dangerous and harsh place full of rough and hard-hearted men and women who could not care less about what you may go through. There is no place for the weak and vulnerable in this world, but for the tough, strong, and fearless. This calls for anyone that feels weak and fearful to seek the help of the strong and fearless.

Sometimes we can find the help we need in our families and sometimes in other Christians, but we can take refuge in God and His infallible word by reading it and praying to Him every day. God is the only refuge we have in times of trouble. Seek him and see for yourself how powerful He is and know that He will hear you when you call on Him. This Psalm sums it up beautifully.

"1. God is our refuge and strength, an ever-present help in trouble. 2. Therefore we will not fear, though the earth give way and the mountains fall into the heart of the sea. (Psalm 46:1-2)

I can say for sure that the Lord has been my refuge and fortress all these years and He is not about to abandon me for anything. He has been faithful, and He will remain forever faithful. Each time feel weak, He gives me strength; when I am afraid, He gives me reassurance; when I am alone, His presence encamps around me. And the list is endless. That is why I love Him with all my heart. This God is a good God. Try Him for yourself. God is a friend that sticks closer than a brother. He does not change like just those friends who keep changing on us now and then. God is constant and we can count on Him. He will never let you down, no matter what."

Chapter 12

My Life in a Nutshell: Highs and Lows

Even though I was born where I lived Zambia for the first 26 years of my life, it was neither my choice nor a mistake. I was born to my two parents who I did not choose, but I loved them when they were alive, and I love them in death. My mother lost her first five children and lost more after my late sister, Doreen. My mother also lost her seventh child as an infant, but my late sister Elizabeth survived.

I came ninth and survived what killed my first six siblings as infants, my two older sisters in their '40s and '50s, my young sister Jenny in her '30s and my lastborn sister Bertha as an infant, I cannot say. That means that my mother lost seven of her eleven children to infant death. I know she did not choose to lose her children, and therefore it must have been hard for her. She must have felt helpless, but she pulled through and brought the four of us up in love and taught us to always have faith in God no matter what, never to revenge, but to forgive and move on and let vengeance be the lords.

I may not understand all this and may not know exactly why I am here, but I cannot make the mistake of thinking I am here to moan and grumble and have pity parties; I cannot afford to have that sort of attitude. There's work to do while God lends me breath.

My mum who lost her husband when he was only 47, in 1976, a budding businessman, an influential local community figure, whose future looked bright and promising. By the time he died, he had played a key role in the building of the very first school for his local community, where he lived after retiring from a national railway company where he worked before embarking on a business life.

What surprises me about my mother's life is that despite losing all those children, and her husband, who was an evangelist, preaching the gospel to everyone, she never blamed God. She honoured, loved, and served Him whole-heartedly until her last breath. How do you explain that sort of attitude? It is unexplainable.

It takes the wisdom and sovereignty of God to manage such matters. Remember, He is God, and He has the final say to every situation. In the dream that I shared in chapter six, it helped me realise it is God who allows and disallows death and death to Him is not a big deal because, when we die, it is not the end. We go to be with Him forever. Death is a sure thing for all humanity regardless of what stage of life it comes at. I thank God for my mother because of her godly attitude and faith in God that I picked up from her. I learnt never to blame God for the adversity of my life, but to trust Him, pray that He would bless me and pray, I do. It is my lifestyle, and it is effective in overcoming challenges of life and maintaining peace and joy.

Over the course of my life, I have faced challenges. On top of losing my dear ones, I have felt rejected and sometimes suspected and wrongly accused of things I would not dream of doing. Why this is the case, I cannot tell, but what I know is that when we all stand before God, He will reveal the truth about us. I have faced tremendous opposition and I have lost money; Jobs have gone just like that, and I have faced racism. Certain individuals hated me along the way, and others have loved me dearly. Friends have called me names and yours may have too. There have been people who wished me ill, but I thank God for all these things because they have made who I am today.

I know such life experiences are common and they are subject to interpretation, but when I look back, I may never have started my journey on the road to recovery had those who rejected and mistreated me had not done so. I may never have learned to trust in Jesus and to learn what true love is. I know, and I have heard other Christians say the same thing which has made me conclude that as long as we are still in this world living in this body of sin, we will face some of these things and therefore we should bible ourselves for them bearing in mind Christ went through worse, but He persevered as the bible puts it in the Hebrews chapter 12:2;

"[2] Fixing our eyes on Jesus, the pioneer and perfecter of faith. For the joy set before him he endured the cross, scorning its shame, and sat down at the right hand of the throne of God." Hebrew 12:2 (NIV)

True love is not just about showing our teeth and telling people who we do not trust what they want to hear to make them feel good, not at all. It is being sincere and telling them, especially if they hurt, the truth even if it hurts. Until the truth comes out, accusers win, but only temporarily. They may be oblivious to their wrongdoing but trying to tackle them is not the answer. It may make things worse and instead of getting the victory, we may appear defensive and make accusers doubt us even more.

That is why I thank those within my social circles that was harsh to me, because I needed that sort of treatment to rise from the dumps where I was at the height of my bereavement. In all this, I can testify that God was with me and saw me through every challenge and gave strength to overcome every hurdle. It is important here to mention that nobody is to blame for the adversity I faced, but God knew it and allowed it to happen for His own reasons.

Again, the last thing I will ever do is blame God. God is too wise as a God to make mistakes. I may never understand why seven of my siblings died in infancy, my dad at 47, my sisters at 30, 40 and 50. Only God knows.

As far as facing rejection goes, people reject other people because of certain reasons. It may be because they find them too demanding, they disagree with them on certain things, they may be jealous, nepotistic, racist, bitter towards them or even someone else, but whatever the case, rejection is subject to interpretation and the reaction that follows makes the difference between how people see us, as well as how we react to the different things they do or say to us. It is like getting affected by it, brushing it aside, and getting on with life.

As far as racism is concerned, it is also possible for racist people to hide it and tread cautiously if the person they are being racist against is brave, no nonsense, likely to stand up to them and let them be. I know it is necessary to choose one's battle, as there may be cases when it may be pointless to speak out, especially in a confrontational and rude manner. This applies to when dealing with relationships and other social issues because that sort of approach makes things worse. Remaining silent and doing nothing about it does not take the problem away, either.

In my case, my fragility because of loss and bereavement got the better of me at times and because I was grieving, I did not negate the need to know how to react to the challenges that came my way no matter what nature the challenges were. For a fact, the people I came across at work, church, college, and other places I went did not know my circumstances and even if they knew, few wanted to make it their business. All they wanted was for me to be brave and get on with life or leave them alone.

I am sorry, but that is exactly what it is. Few people want to leave their homes to attend events just to find themselves dealing with your grief. Even if they did, there's risk that they may not make a job excellent job of it.

Most people want to go out and have an enjoyable time. Whatever they did on each occasion, whether it be shopping, sightseeing, eating out, and other activities. I wish I learnt this lesson early enough because I may have saved myself from experiencing the pain I felt when I did not get the pampering and the tender and loving care that I expected, especially from fellow Christians.

In hindsight, I am glad that no one pampered me, although I am sad that I did not feel supported when I needed it the most. However, I now know I cannot blame anyone for it. Not everyone has the gift of comforting others, especially if it is not their official or formal role.

This then means that people who need bereavement counselling should seek the help of qualified counsellors and seek the support of pastors for spiritual inspiration and prayer. There is room for spiritual support in other Christians, especially those that would have gone through similar circumstances because experience is the best teacher. No wonder the bibles talks about comforting others with the comfort we have received in 2 Corinthians 1:3–4 where it is written;

"[3] Praise be to the God and Father of our Lord Jesus Christ, the Father of compassion and the God of all comfort, [4] who comforts us in all our troubles, so that we can comfort those in any trouble with the comfort we ourselves receive from God." 2 Corinthians 1:2–4 (NIV)

What a beautiful and uplifting verse. I can imagine that the people who showed me kindness and comforted me knew something of this verse or were just sensitive to the leading of the Holy Spirit because there were many more that stood by me, prayed for me, encouraged me, and showed me Christian love and patience. I have found favour in the sight of God and men and have seen doors open in the most unusual of ways.

A good example is how an agency job I got became a saviour each time a major job came to a sudden end, and yes, jobs have ended, both because I was no longer needed and constructive dismissal; kicked out or because I knew within me, I had outlived my welcome and usefulness in the organisation. So, I needed to trust God for the next job and move on. But when that happened, this agency job tidied me until God opened another door.

I did not know that God, who holds the future, connected me to a wonderful family to supervise their mother during a showering session after having a fall when she tried doing it on her own; that and my connection with an 87-year-old lady who I have known for over ten years was God-ordained to keep me financially stable. This lady's family was such a lovely and supportive family to her.

I collaborated well with them. They always showed me appreciation and treated me with respect. I could not have asked for a better family to have connections with. I thank God for them. All this is because despite experiencing loss and bereavement so many times over, it does not give me my own exclusive terms and conditions for living. As already mentioned, I still need to work, earn a living, and pay bills; this goes for everyone else going through bereavement. Life goes on.

As far as work is concerned, I could not take it for granted each time I needed a job, but had to look for one, prepare for interviews and so by God's grace and hard work, I have done job roles I could never have dreamt of ever being given. The most outstanding one was when was my appointment to the position of service manager prior to completing the management course relevant to the role. All this is because of God's grace and favour that made Him to navigate my career path by bringing the right people my way. I see it as God channelling His love for me through people and therefore, I can testify that, there have been many people in my life who have accepted and loved me. I have known God's enabling grace and have proved that God is a present help in times of need. He has touched me and healed me when I have needed it and he has used the most unlikely circumstances to turn adverse circumstances around for my good.

There is no language that can suffice in expressing the goodness of God. He is simply a wonderful, loving, and merciful God. I love Him with all my soul, spirit, and body. To endeavour to live for God for the rest of my days. I hope that reading my story has blessed you somehow.

I have authored this book to prove to the reader that problems are a part of life. And so is death. As humans, we face problems of different magnitudes, and these affect us in diverse ways. Death comes to everyone; it is no respecter of people; the rich, the poor, the black, white, yellow, brown, the young, old, middle-aged, they all die. It is down to those who remain to move on. It is difficult, but time is a healer. Those who are lucky may have had kind and patient people around them and this helps to bring healing. Disagreements happen between people of all backgrounds, political, religious affiliations, ethnic origins, and social classes. They are a part of life. People disagree for varied reasons and different people react to disagreements in diverse ways. It is better, as the saying goes, 'To let the bygones be bygones rather than keep grudges.'

They say that the consequences of bearing grudges have a more devastating effect on the bitter person than it has on the happy-go-lucky person. When you bear a grudge, and this is regardless of whether you are in right or wrong, you are poisoning yourself and could end up with a line that may even lead you to the grave when you are young.

Misunderstandings happen wherever you find people living alongside one another, at home, at school, at work and at other places where humans mingle. These happen not only between people of different ethnic origins, different social classes, or different families. They can happen between people from one family, from the same ethnicity, political affiliation, and religious beliefs. They are bound to happen when there is over one human being existing side by side.

If you have been involved in any of the above, it does not mean that there is something wrong with you. It does not always mean that you are the worst person if you find yourself in any of the above situations. Even dying early is not because those who have gone ahead have sinned or that they were bad people. It is because nobody controls their lives. We may all know that one day we will leave the face of the earth, but nobody knows when. Living in peace and avoiding confrontation is the best way to live with others. There is no benefit from wanting your own way or being divisive and stirring up trouble.

I can imagine that those who cause trouble or even take other people's lives have no peace. The world would be such a peaceful place if everyone understood that all life is special and living in peace is the best way to leave together regardless of race, skin colour, social status, religious beliefs, or political affiliation. It is fair to say that most people who perpetrate trouble are unhappy within themselves. It would be interesting to know what they are like in their own homes. They could make trouble even for their own family and friends who must cope with living with these bitter and angry people who may even take anger and bitterness out on their friends and family.

It seems to me as if no one can help people like these. They therefore need to sort themselves out before it is too late.

The day of reckoning will come and that is when they will wish they never did what they did to hurt others. The price they may pay could be dear and there may be no amount of apology and regret that can switch time back.

Life is what you make of it. No one is immune to the challenges of life. The only difference is that the nature and extent of challenges faced depend on individual circumstances. For example, certain people who have all the money they need in the world, but they may have disease in their bodies and because, in a general sense, money does not buy health, their money is useless in the light of an incurable disease. Others may be in good health, but they may be poor because of no fault in their own body or even because of losing their job for whatever reason.

There are people who always look for someone to blame for their problems and they take it out on them. For example, there are people who think that they cannot find jobs because foreigners have taken all the jobs and yet in most cases foreigners take those jobs that no one wants to do. There are cultures, especially the Africa culture, people blame magic or witchcraft for their lack of success and for illnesses. I find this incredibly sad.

If witches are that powerful, are they more powerful than God? Are they behind every problem those who put everything down to witchcraft go through? The fact it, it is possible for things to go wrong for unexplained reasons and the best thing in such cases is to devote time in trying to find the root cause and to work out a plan to solve the issue or overcome the challenge. The only most important thing you can do if you believe in God is to pray earnestly as ask other believers to pray behind you. It is a proven fact that prayer changes things. My life is proof that prayer changes things because God answers prayer made in Jesus's name, if there is no doubt. My faith works for me and that is how I have overcome grief and can laugh and enjoy the company of others without feeling left out or allowing bitterness to ruin my life any further.